Future-proof Your Business

Tom Cheesewright is an applied futurist, helping people and organizations around the world to see the future more clearly, share their vision and respond with innovation. An accomplished speaker and broadcaster, he specializes in connecting tomorrow's world to today's experience, making sense of what's happening next, and why. Tom's clients include global 500 corporations, government departments, industry bodies and charities. Notable clients include: Accenture, Audi, Bacardi, Barclays, BASF, Bertelsmann, BMW, BP, BT, Facebook, Google, HSBC, HMRC, ITV, Kellogg's, Sony, Virgin Media and Visa. Tom's first book, *High Frequency Change*, was published in June 2019.

Tom Cheesewright

Future-proof Your Business

BUSINESS

PENGUIN BOOKS

UK | USA | Canada | Ireland | Australia
India | New Zealand | South Africa

Penguin Books is part of the Penguin Random
House group of companies whose addresses can
be found at global.penguinrandomhouse.com.

Penguin
Random House
UK

First published 2020
001

Copyright © Tom Cheesewright, 2020

The moral right of the author has been asserted

Text design by Richard Marston
Set in 11.75/14.75 pt Minion Pro
Typeset by Jouve (UK), Milton Keynes
Printed and bound in Great Britain by
Clays Ltd, Elcograf S.p.A.

A CIP catalogue record for this book is available
from the British Library

ISBN: 978-0-241-44644-7

Follow us on LinkedIn: linkedin.com/
company/penguin-connect/
www.greenpenguin.co.uk

Contents

Introduction

Let me start with a nightmare. Imagine you are driving down the motorway at speed and you lose control of your car. You realize that your accelerator pedal is stuck and your brakes have stopped working. As your speed increases, cars and trucks start rushing towards you, and you begin to swerve across the road as you try desperately to avoid a collision. Your adrenaline levels skyrocket, panic rises and survival strategies whir through your brain at lightning speed. One wrong move now could be catastrophic.

What is going to keep you alive?

This is the scenario that every leader in business faces today. We are all operating in an age of high-frequency change. Overlaid on existing large, multi-decade trends are many small, fast waves of change enabled by a globalized market and the friction-lowering effect of technology. These high-frequency waves carry rapid shifts in everything from consumer products to popular culture, and from corporate systems to customer attitudes. Their effects tend to be narrow, touching just one sector or industry, or even a single company. But within those narrow bounds they can be extremely disruptive. Business people around the world are finding that the pace of this change is accelerating; more obstacles are appearing and creating an increasingly complex landscape in which to manage a successful business, both now and in the future.

So, how do you survive?

The phenomenon of high-frequency change has forced organizations from BMW to the British government to think differently about how they do business, and in doing so they have often called on me for advice. This book contains the distilled lessons that I have learned while working with many different organizations on the challenges they face in preparing for the future. This is my tried and tested method for changing the outlook, behaviour and even shape of any business to prepare it for the uncertainty of tomorrow.

The book is structured around the three core characteristics of future-ready organizations, characteristics that are very similar to those we see in the world's best athletes.

Top sports stars shape their bodies for the challenges facing them. They build the agility and strength they require for their discipline. They are limber and supple, and able to show resilience in the face of sometimes punishing competition. You will similarly need to build a culture of agility within your own organization. You will learn in this book how to reshape your business for an age where adaptability to tomorrow's challenge is a better predictor of success than being perfectly optimized to today's conditions.

Successful athletes have both a profound sense of their immediate environment and great strategic awareness. They can read the game before anyone else and translate that understanding into winning action. Think about the racing driver with an almost sixth sense about the positions of their competitors behind them. Think about the marathon runner knowing exactly when to make their break. Or the footballer able to make that defence-splitting diagonal pass, placing the ball on the boot of the winger who they just know will be running forward to receive it. Foresight like this is a skill of fundamental importance to leaders. In this book you will learn to hone your ability to spot potential obstacles before they arise. The further off you can identify issues, the more chance you have of preparing yourself, steering your organization towards safety and staying in control of your operational environment.

Winning athletes process information quickly and make the right decisions. They absorb the rich information from their senses and map out the possibilities that their foresight presents. Then they make a decision and take action – fast. You must do the same, accelerating the flow of useful information through your business and speeding the response to external stimuli.

These three characteristics – agility, awareness and action – are visible in the most future-proof businesses. I call such businesses Athletic Organizations. Use the proven tools in this book and you can make your organization more athletic. Each of the three parts addresses one of the three characteristics.

The first part of this book is about the structure of your business. About getting fit, like the athlete, and sufficiently agile to face the challenges ahead. Just as a better-handling car would give you the greatest chance of survival in the motorway scenario with which I began, a more agile business is better equipped to respond to future shocks. Business leaders around the world know that the future is more uncertain now than ever. They know that their business models may have a shorter shelf life than they would have had ten or twenty years ago. So, they are changing the structure of their businesses to make them more agile. Instead of optimizing for today's reality, they are building businesses that can adapt constantly for more sustainable success. In Part 1, I will explain the fundamentals of structuring a business that can be continually reconfigured to meet changing market demands.

The second part of this book is about developing awareness and foresight, just like the athlete learning to read the game. You need to be clear what is likely to happen in the immediate future, the near future, and beyond. This is something that most companies do very poorly. Including foresight tools and processes as part of your day-to-day management activity will give your organization an immediate advantage. It does not have to be time-consuming and it does not have to be expensive. But it does have to be consistent. Forward planning is not something that can be thought about every five or ten years any more. It is an activity that must be conducted at least twice a year. In Part 2, I will explain different approaches for looking to the future, and suggest how and when you use them to give your company the clearest picture of tomorrow.

Foresight is only valuable if the visions of the future that you see are translated into action today. So, the final part of this book will look at the different ways to enhance your decision-making. As organizations grow, they tend to centralize power, build bureaucracy and slow the flow of information. In the words of Howard Dresner, the man who coined the term 'business intelligence', future-ready organizations must be 'hyper-decisive'. In Part 3, I will show how you can accelerate decision-making in your organization, making it much more receptive to immediate signals from customers and the market, and to the strategic responses you develop to future visions.

This book is for people who lead businesses, or who aspire to. For people with management responsibility for the whole or part of an organization, or who are in a senior executive role in one of its functions. It is not aimed at start-ups, though it may inform their development, but at established organizations with anywhere from tens to tens of thousands of employees. Companies that have established a pattern of success but now recognize that it is necessary to make changes if that success is to be sustained.

No business is truly future-proof. Sometimes the scale of the shocks that come are simply too great to be survived. But few business leaders even see the shocks coming until it is too late. When they come, they are ill-equipped to respond. The aim of this book is to give you the best chance of seeing the future shocks that are coming your way, and to give you the tools to respond faster than your competitors. I cannot guarantee that your business will be the one to survive and thrive, but I can help you to improve the odds dramatically.

Part 1 How to Structure a Future-proof Business

Future-proofing your business means turning it into an Athletic Organization. And the first step to building an Athletic Organization is to get it into shape. But what shape should that be?

In this section I will describe how changing the shape of the business starts with a change in mindset. How we must reset our own expectations about what leadership looks like, as we move from an age of constant optimization to an age where adaptation is a much better predictor of success.

Based on this understanding, how can we build businesses – especially large, complex ones – that are well equipped for rapid adaptation? It can be done, and I will show you how.

But first, we start with why. Why are the rules of success so different in the future from those in the past?

1.1 Optimization vs Adaptation

Leading an established business is all about optimization. Or at least, it long has been.

In an ideal world, as a leader you don't work *in* the business on day-to-day delivery. Your job is to work *on* the business to increase returns, one way or another. Grow revenues, cut costs – whatever you must do, you need to tune the engine of the business to peak performance.

The timespan over which your success as a leader is measured against these expectations has declined. You are expected to deliver today. Everyone is focused on the next reporting period, whether it is the next quarter or the year end. If the numbers are heading in the wrong direction, you are likely to be gone soon afterwards. In the US, almost half of CEOs of large organizations stay in post less than five years.[1] In fact, five years is the average tenure, down a full 20 per cent since 2013. The UK is no different. In FTSE100 companies, the average CEO tenure is also just five years,[2] even if the speed of turnover has fallen very slightly of late. It seems the only leaders on a more uncertain footing than CEOs are football managers. Or maybe the leaders of political parties.

The result of this extreme short-termism and focus on immediate results is that, in most organizations, there is little scope for leaders to focus on the future. The objective is not sustainable success but immediate success.

This shapes leaders' behaviour, blinding them to opportunities beyond the scope of day-to-day operations. And it shapes the organization itself. Every asset and every process is progressively honed to maximize returns over the near term. The business becomes a machine optimized for the work that it does today, not for what the customer might require tomorrow.

This is where the problem lies. This approach may well deliver results in the short term. It may be the means by which the company has achieved its current success. It may even leave some leaders with healthy bonuses before they inevitably find themselves moving on. But it is ultimately a recipe for disaster.

In an age of high-frequency change, that disaster looms ever closer.

High-frequency change is a relatively new phenomenon affecting people and organizations today. It is the result of globalization combined with the lowering of friction in business enabled by high-speed digital-communications technologies. Together, these two factors have produced fast-moving waves of change that appear on the near horizon and flow through an industry or company. In a low-friction environment it is possible to develop, scale and distribute many things more quickly than before, from ideas and memes to software and hardware, consumer products and services.

These waves of high-frequency change tend not to have broad impacts; they won't transform every aspect of our lives. (Big cross-societal changes that do this, like the introduction of the affordable motor car or the development of the connected computer, still take decades to have their effect.) But inside narrowly defined sectors, high-frequency change can be utterly disruptive. The result is that the lifespan of products and services, and the business on which they are based, is declining. Leaders are therefore suddenly forced to rethink their approaches to development. A successful 'moon shot' (a radical change in business model) might be required not in the next couple of decades but the next couple of years.

Moving with the times

Businesses that did not keep up with changing times have always failed. The coach builders who didn't make the leap from pony power to the internal combustion engine were left behind. But that was a transition that took decades. Today, businesses can be completely undermined by a high-frequency change that appears on the near horizon and takes effect in just a few months.

Avoiding this fate takes more than just foresight and accelerated decision-making, the facilities highlighted in Parts 2 and 3 of this book. It takes a readiness to act. Building that readiness means changing the very structure of the business to refocus it from absolute optimization to ultimate agility.

What does this new structure look like? No item is more overused in analogies than the humble Lego brick. I acknowledge this as a pre-emptive request for forgiveness for the cliché that follows. Because I have yet to find a better way of explaining the difference between being adaptable and being optimal than the comparison between a die-cast toy car and a Lego model of the same vehicle.

A tale of two toys

Imagine that you give a child a die-cast toy car at Christmas. She is obsessed with Ferraris, so you give her a beautiful model of the classic Testarossa. With its deep red sheen and perfectly modelled body, it is an exact replica of the real thing, right down to the fluted side pods, scaled steering wheel and sports seats inside. It is, you might say, optimized.

The toy Testarossa is fun to play with, for a time. What it cannot do, though, is hold the child's attention for very long. Sometime in the next few hours, days or weeks she will tire of the car scudding across the kitchen floor and over tables, and move on to something new. The car cannot change to meet her new interests. At least not without major metal surgery, the application of an angle grinder or liberal amounts of superglue.

Imagine, instead, that the car was made of Lego. This model is not optimized. It does not have the same sleek lines or accurate internal details. It is still recognizably a Testarossa, but it is an approximation, sheathed in knobbly bits that allow it to hold together. The car still rolls along the floors and furniture in a pleasing fashion. But critically, when the child tires of this simple game, the Lego Ferrari can be ripped apart and reassembled into something new. What was a supercar can become a speedboat or a spaceship, a lion or a dinosaur. This transformation takes a fraction of the energy and time that it would take to similarly transform the die-cast car. Within a few minutes, the same functional blocks can be reassembled into a form that is recognizably a new model.

An agile business, ready to transform to meet changing demands from customers and the market, is one that is assembled from the corporate equivalent of Lego bricks. Just like the Lego car, it will not be as optimized as its sleek, die-cast peer. It will be less efficient, and therefore most likely less profitable. The corporate equivalents of the knobbly bits have a cost, an overhead. But this business assembled from building blocks will be much more resilient. Much more able to weather changes in the economy, trends and customer demands. And it will be capable of extending more quickly into new markets and services.

So, companies and their leaders have a choice. Do you want to be hyper-optimized for today's environment? Or do you want to be agile so that you can adapt to tomorrow's? You cannot be both.

If you have your eye on long-term success, on a legacy of a sustainable business, then read on.

1.2 Stratification

How do you get from an analogy to a strategy to a formal approach? Any framework for business transformation must be somewhat loose if it is to be broadly applicable to a wide range of business types and sizes. But the approach I will lay out here, stratification, provides an overarching template for what a future-proof and agile business might look like.

I began to develop the stratification model in the wake of the 2008 financial crash. During the subsequent cuts in government investment, every UK local authority had to find enormous savings, in many cases losing 50 per cent or more of their resources. The CEO of one such authority approached me. He had recruited a consultancy to help him to restructure the organization to meet its newly constrained budget. He knew that by following the strict advice of his consultants, they would reach a point where it could operate, but he also knew that the organization that would emerge from that exercise would be far different from one structured from first principles to meet the demands of the modern environment. So that was the task he set me: design a local authority from scratch for the twenty-first century.

Contrary to popular belief, there are few differences between a modern local authority and any well-established mid-to-large-sized corporation. Both suffer from ageing technology, sometimes rancorous internal politics, organically grown bureaucracy, and complex communications and management structures. Both are frequently held together by the efforts of great people who make these issues almost invisible by dint of their ingenuity and hard work. After redesigning the local authority, I quickly learned that the framework and principles we created were just as applicable in the private sector. And over time these principles have been progressively revised, mostly through interactions with corporations.

Getting to grips with the stratification framework starts with the understanding of a basic tenet: that in the future, networks will always beat monoliths.

Networks beat monoliths

In the past, if you were trying to make an organization more efficient it made sense to connect all the moving parts as closely as possible. This meant putting different functions under the same roof, whether that roof was a physical one, with people in the same building, or a legal one, with people housed in the same operating entity. Here the barriers to communication and interaction could be minimized. Everyone was notionally working towards the same end. There was little contractual complication beyond employment law as to who was going to do precisely what. And most of us at some point in our careers have gone above and beyond what was contractually required in order to ensure the success of the business and contribute to the progress of our own careers.[3]

The growth in outsourcing during the late 1990s and 2000s showed the value of this approach but also presaged its decline. Through the dotcom boom, capital-rich companies brought online vast amounts of telecommunications infrastructure. This dramatically reduced the friction in global communications. With documents and processes increasingly digitized, it became easier to send administrative and customer services processes offshore for cheaper handling. Many countries had ready supplies of young, highly educated labour ready to take on these tasks.

It seemed like an ideal fit, and it was a strategy pursued aggressively by many corporations. But much of the outsourcing done throughout this period was driven by pure cost optimization.[4] It should be no surprise, therefore, that when the work was done by remote workers being paid less, its quality often fell. Based outside the corporate shell, and with limited incentives, these people were inevitably less aligned to the values of the brand they represented, whether they were part of accounts payable or customer services. With so many layers of contractual bureaucracy between them and the ultimate client, they were disconnected.

Nonetheless, during this period many companies were able to offload activities that were not at the core of their success. What they found, for the most part, was that if the process was handled well and the integration between the company outsourcing a function and the company taking it on was well designed, then there was very little friction in communication. No longer did it necessarily make sense to house all the functions inside the same legal entity, let alone the same physical building or even the same country.

The combination of improved digital technologies and a shared global culture, underpinned by the internet, had created a new environment. One where you could grow a successful business by developing capabilities associated only with your core value proposition. Everything else could be bought in, on demand.

This trend took another leap forward with the widespread sharing of APIs (application programming interfaces) in the second wave of the web, known as Web 2.0. APIs are a means of simply allowing two pieces of software to communicate without a human presence. Starting from the early 2000s, large web-based companies such as Salesforce and eBay began to open up the APIs to their products, allowing other people to build things on top of them, and use their data and services – sometimes for free and sometimes for a fee. This allowed these companies and others to create a huge ecosystem of applications that relied on their core proposition. This improved their own proposition and created a plethora of new routes to attracting customers. All without them investing in developing niche propositions that were beyond their core business. The same was true of the companies building tools on top of these platforms: they no longer needed to build much of the 'back end' – the boring stuff that the customer never sees but is necessary for the product to work. Instead, they could just add a thin layer of value on top of the existing proposition. It is this layering of value that first led me to the name 'stratification', and, as you will come to see, the concept of layers is very important in this model.

Today you can find a whole host of apps for researching the eBay marketplace, creating and managing listings. The Salesforce AppExchange offers thousands of apps for managing contracts, marketing, customer onboarding and more. Every one of these large software platforms has its own, often overlapping, ecosystem of smaller suppliers.

More and more digital-first companies began to take on the type of work that the big outsourcers had offered to handle in the 1990s. They could now receive instruction via API rather than a phone call or a fax. Documents could be routed automatically to other companies for specialist pieces of software, or sometimes teams of human beings, to each fulfil their own small function.

Take the accounting processes for my business today as a very small-scale example. Every time I spend some money in my business, I take a photo of the receipt and send it to my receipt processing app, ReceiptBank, where a computer uses optical character recognition (OCR) software to read the receipt and insert the details into my cloud-based accounting program, Xero. Humans handle only the exceptions.

Much of the time, I don't even have to take a picture of the receipt. For frequent online purchases such as train tickets, my email platform, Google, recognizes that I have received a receipt and automatically forwards it to ReceiptBank. Once a month my outsourced bookkeeper sends me an email with a cloud document that includes all his questions about the transactions. These are the exceptions where the automated system hasn't quite worked or, more likely, I have failed to add a receipt. There are usually fewer than ten exceptions in total and it takes me a matter of minutes to update the cloud document. My accountant is notified that I have made the changes and the accounts are updated accordingly.

Processes like this are now happening around the world at enormous scale, stripping further friction from the outsourcing process and leading me to one obvious conclusion. With a few critical exceptions there is no longer a clear operational advantage to maintaining anything except your core functions under the same legal umbrella. There might be other reasons to do so, as I will go on to show, but a networked operation like the one I've described can be incredibly efficient.

One of the advantages of a network is flexibility. The old outsourcing contracts were complex, multi-year affairs. People were likely to expend huge legal and consulting fees getting out of them when they failed, having spent just as much getting into them in the first place. Today, outsourcing can be an entirely different proposition because the cost and complexity of routing digitized work, whether it is calls, documents or digital processes, is now so much lower. Of course, large and complex outsourcing arrangements still exist, but many networked business arrangements can be created, or collapsed, much more quickly than before.

That is not to say that the networked business doesn't pose challenges. For example, how do you ensure quality and consistency? What happens when a partner shuts down unexpectedly? How do you deal with changes to the APIs via which you integrate with other services?

Part of the answer to these questions is not to outsource at all but to construct your business as if it is a group of loosely coupled functions that outsource to each other. To build it as a box of Lego bricks, not a die-cast car. The same advantages of agility apply, even if all the functional units exist under the same legal umbrella. This has been the finding of some companies pursuing a 'shared services' approach.

Structuring for agility: shared services

The Shared Services Forum UK brings together diverse organizations all working towards the same goal: unifying fractured and distributed functions across a business into a coherent whole. For example, you might bring together all the HR or finance functions across a business into a single unit. Once you've done that there might be some obvious cost savings, but more important are the opportunities for process improvement, entrepreneurship and agility.

One coherent block is much easier to manipulate when you need to change the structure of the business to meet future needs. It also presents a single proposition if you wanted to make this service market-facing. Great at HR or finance? Why not do it for other, similar organizations or different parts of the same group? The reverse is true too: why not use someone else's function if it can neatly be plugged into your own systems?

> *The perception of shared services has been primarily about cost savings, but companies that have really pursued this model have found much greater benefits. Shared services creates a level of transparency in the business that reduces friction, making it wholly more adaptable and focused.*
> Lisa (Hooley) Edwards, Evolve Collaboration, and Board Director, Shared Services Forum UK.

The shared services model is not a silver bullet. As Lisa notes, the driver behind this move is often cost saving, and that can lead to business decisions that do not promote agility, for example the over-centralization of power. For shared services to be a future-proof approach, it must be undertaken with the right motivation and mindset. Functions must be given entrepreneurial freedom, and the interfaces between these services and the rest of the organization need to be very well designed to minimize friction. In short, if you are trying to move to a shared services model for purely financial reasons, then you are back in an optimization mindset, not focused on growing agility.

Good people and bad organizations

Every business is a mixture of both insourced and outsourced functions. It just depends on where you draw the boundaries of what is 'your' business. Think about your business having interfaces on each side. Upstream there is your supply chain. Downstream there are your sales and distribution channels. On one side there are your financial partners, banks and investors. On the other, your support services in marketing, law and auditing. Without these partners, do you really have a business? So, when you are drawing the boundaries of your business, how much do you include?

The critical challenge for building agility is ensuring that wherever these functions sit, they are structured for flexibility. And this places particular emphasis on the interfaces between them. Understanding the inputs and outputs for each function and ensuring the smooth flow of information between them determines much of your organization's ability to change. It is the breakdown of this communication that often makes it necessary for people to step up to span the gaps.

Good people will always overcome poor processes to keep the cogs turning. They will often do this for months or even years before they raise a flag to say that something is broken. Sometimes they never say anything. They just come to treat dealing with a broken process as part of their job. But this is dangerous. It is why I say that good people are one of the biggest risks to organizations. Because they hide structural failures. And good people are always in demand elsewhere. When they leave to take up a better offer, or simply because of the stress, things can fall apart rapidly.

Good people covering for bad processes also make

organizations opaque. It is hard to analyse processes when they exist in someone's head. It makes organizations harder to manage and even harder to change when they are reliant on informal information flows that exist undocumented and survive only on the efforts and goodwill of a few individuals. This is not a future-proof approach.

You want good people in your organization, obviously. But relying on their efforts to see you through without the support of good processes will not deliver sustainable success. Ensure that you have a culture where people are confident to speak out when they come across a bad process, or particularly a bad interface. Give them confidence that it will be addressed.

How do you do this? As a leader you must seek out criticism and challenge, and demonstrate that it will be listened to and dealt with:

- Create formal opportunities for people to give feedback about broken processes, anonymously if they prefer.
- Qualify the issues raised by speaking to other people in the same role. Do they all have a similar experience?
- If so, then quantify the issues to understand the scale of their impact.
- Using this information you can make a clear business case for investment.

Whatever the outcome of your investigation, feed everything back to the team. Be completely transparent: you have looked at the issues, weighed up the evidence and made a decision. This will give people confidence to keep feeding back, reinforcing the culture of communication.

1.3 Building Blocks

Today, most large or established businesses are monolithic. They will have partners and some outsourced functions, whether they are component suppliers, auditors or logistics handlers. But most companies fulfil lots of functions under the same legal umbrella: finance, HR, marketing. Stratification is about transforming this monolithic block into a network and the first step is to begin identifying what the individual blocks might be.

What are your building blocks?

What is the smallest reducible unit of your business? What does a corporate building block look like? Understand this and you can identify the individual nodes in your newly networked business.

In many ways, each of these building blocks is a business in its own right. We will map it out in a similar way to how one might plan out a start-up, using a tool similar to Alexander Osterwalder's Business Model Canvas that has been the beginning of so many successful start-ups.[5] Like a start-up, your building blocks will be much simpler than an established business with all its legacy and complexity. Each building block fulfils one clearly definable function that takes inputs, returns outputs and that can be measured in terms of its performance. A building block is defined by its function.

This sounds very simple and, in many cases, it can be. But what is simple in theory is often complicated in practice, especially where ideas meet an established organizational chart and real human beings. Particularly in smaller organizations, one person may have multiple roles or be responsible for multiple functions. It is hard to divide that person down into neat chunks. But what we are looking to divide up here is the *processes* rather than the *people*.

Capturing core functions

What is a core function? What is a piece of work that can be neatly described here? Each one is what you might think of as a product or service. Something that you could describe neatly so that you could sell it to someone else. Let us start with an example that is already frequently outsourced: delivery. You pay someone to take an object from you, to a destination you define, with a level of care and other restrictions that you can also specify.

What about an example from inside the business? How about recruitment? You might ask HR to return candidates against a job specification. HR might then task a recruitment agency with this brief. How about expenses processing? Or procurement? These are all insourced functions that have frequently been repackaged for outsourcing, so that we know they can be captured as clear functions.

Each of these processes, and indeed every process in a business, has inputs and outputs wrapped around its core function. Identifying these and the core process itself is the starting point for breaking your organization down into functional units.

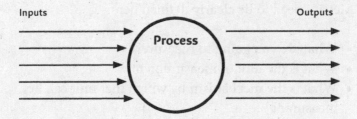

What might the inputs and outputs be? Here are some examples:

Input	Output
Customer inquiry	Resolution of customer inquiry
Supplier invoice	Payment
Shipping order	Picked and packed order

The inputs and outputs are the points at which the function interfaces with the rest of the business. These are the bits that stick the business together. But they cannot be the only interface, there needs to be some transparency about what is going on inside the function. A management interface. This is where the metrics come in: what can you measure about the operation of this function that tells you whether it is performing well or not?

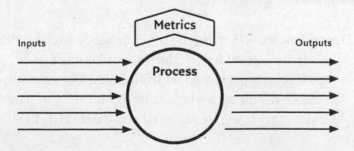

Metrics need to be clearly defined here.

- What are you going to measure?
- What is the unit of measurement?
- What is the mechanism by which that unit can be measured?

The aim is to gain some insight into the operations of what might be distant and remote functions, sufficient to know at a high level whether it is operating well or whether there is a problem. You do not want to measure too much and you do not want the task of reporting to affect the function onerously.

Ideally, any metrics should be an intrinsic part of the day-to-day activities, extracted automatically from the unit's operational systems. The only caveat to this is to ensure that what is being measured translates to or at least correlates with value. Throughput alone is often a poor measure. As is price, as anyone will know who has watched price-incentivized procurement functions chase ever lower costs, to the point where what they're buying is not fit for purpose. The key thing is to map the outputs of the function back to the desired outcomes for the business: how does what they are doing affect what you want the business to achieve?

To complete the picture of this functional unit, we need to ask some more questions of it:

Dependencies: What are the other dependencies for this unit in its current form? The things that don't sit as inputs or outputs but on which it relies? For example, it could be reliant on a whole suite of internal company services that could be captured as a block: HR, IT, premises, etc. It might also rely on some critical external suppliers, whether that's software, services or perhaps a connection to an organization like HMRC. Maybe it is already reliant on some outsourcing to complete its core function?

Competitors: Who else could complete this function? Who does, either inside or outside the business? Is this something that has natural outsourcing partners, such as a marketing agency, BPO (Business Process Outsourcing) provider or a fully software-driven automation?

Direct customers: If this function were a service or product in its own right, would there be potential customers for it? They might be inside the company, inside the wider group or fully external customers. Who are they? And is there a market there? Clue: the presence of an existing and competitive marketplace is a positive not a negative. Someone has already proved the business model and educated the market about its value.

Cost attribution: How is this unit paid for? Does it contribute directly to the value of goods or services? What proportion of the final service or product price for your company as a whole is made up of the costs for this function?

Revenue model: If this function were to charge, either internal cross-charging or for its services, what would that look like? What would the pricing unit be?

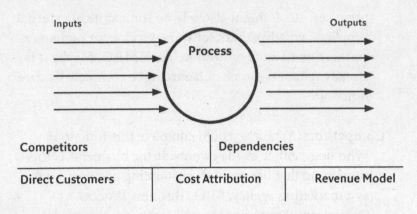

Where units break down

Completing the unit templates shown in the diagrams often highlights a number of issues for a business. These are some things to look out for:

Lack of metrics: I frequently find that leaders and managers have no effective way of measuring the performance of different units within the organization. This is particularly true of organizations where budget or profit has not been an issue: often, while there is money available, few hard questions are asked. Establishing metrics and a means of capturing and displaying them is hugely important and can be positive for all parties, allowing leaders to manage by exception and giving units and unit heads a much clearer focus. The risk is that the selected metrics or means of measurement are wrong, skewing the incentive away from real business goals.

Lack of coherence: In the 1990s, the anthropologist Robin Dunbar suggested there was a limit to the number of stable social relationships a human can maintain. As soon as organizations scale beyond the 'Dunbar number' of around 150 people, organizations start to lose coherence. Units start to stray from the core business goals and individuals lose sight of why they do what they do. As I often find myself pointing out, no one comes into work and looks at their job description. Instead, they do what they did yesterday plus or minus a few per cent. Over time this adds up to complete misalignment: a lack of coherence.

Lack of cost clarity: Profitable or well-funded organizations are particularly bad at recognizing where their costs lie, or their real sources of profit. Once you start to assess them on a unit basis it becomes clear that business costs have not been properly attributed and nor have profits been associated to the services that customers really value.

Humans and machines

The importance of separating processes from people is illustrated when you start to examine the next phase of outsourcing: handing work to autonomous machines. There are many conversations about the future of work and whether robots will take our jobs. But robots do not take jobs. Human beings are incredibly complex and flexible. Almost every job involves a range of different activities: interpreting instructions, communicating with co-workers, answering inquiries. A robot might be able to do one of these functions, maybe even the core one, whether it is reconciling numbers or putting spot welds into a car body. But one robot is unlikely to be able to complete all the others successfully as well.

Instead of taking jobs, robots take work. They typically each fulfil one function, one part of the many tasks that take up the working day. Rarely will one robot be a direct replacement for one person. Instead, one robot might do 20 or 30 per cent of all the work done by a team of people, the result being that you might then shrink that team by 20 or 30 per cent.

With growing possibilities for robotic automation and human augmentation with technology, we must improve our understanding of the work that our people do. Without this knowledge, we will never understand where in the workplace humans add enormous value and where machines are the better choice. Indeed, we will never understand how to release our people from administration and drudgery to deliver more value.

Sometimes, in following the procedure, you might find it hard to capture a process currently undertaken by a human in a form that could be replicated by a machine or outsourced to a third party. This can mean one of two things. It could be that this hard-to-describe process or function is extremely valuable, or it could be that it is of no value at all. Give both options equal consideration and don't jump to conclusions. Not everything will neatly fit the framework, and some of those things might be critical to your success.

Note also that conducting this exercise is not automatically a step towards outsourcing. There are often advantages to owning and operating these units and there are structures, such as shared services, that enable this to be done in a more flexible framework. But those advantages should be clear and visible.

Without this level of depth and insight the performance of each unit is often hidden within the monolithic whole.

Mapping to units

In any organization of scale, the process of mapping functions to units would be a near-Sisyphean task.[6] It represents the type of 'big bang' change that can consume an organization for years, often not to the best ends. Instead, for any established organization, this should be a process that is progressive, shared and iterative.

By progressive I mean it is not done all at once, but that begs the question of where to start. The answer is with those places that present a challenge. In the chapters that follow, I will help you identify pressure points in your business. These will be a good place to start. By shared, I mean that the unitization of each function should be undertaken by the people leading that function. If imposed from outside, ideas about inputs and outputs, and particularly metrics, can seem like a burden on the team in question. Allow them to define their function more clearly and it can be a valuable exercise in clarifying thinking and shifting people away from their worn-in processes and business-as-usual mindset.

1.4 The Ring Model

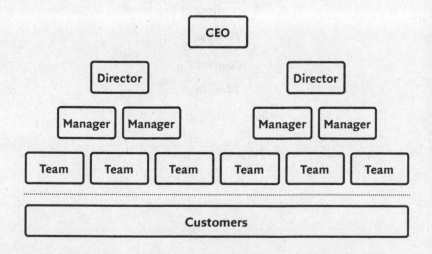

Once you have broken a business down into building blocks, how do you then reassemble it into a complete operation? Most business diagrams end up being hierarchical, often placing the customer right at the bottom of this hierarchy.

I suggest an alternative approach. When working with clients, I've found that it is helpful to think about the business being broken down into a series of concentric rings. The rings in this case are defined by a coherence of purpose and the need for co-ordination across them, be that through language, design or data. Placing functions into the relevant rings helps to identify opportunities to reduce friction, whether that is the duplication of effort internally or the elimination of friction between business and the customer.

It is the customer who sits at the centre of all the rings. This visualization helps to focus the mind.

Some units might span two or three rings. Layers may not all be constructed of wholly owned units: some will be supplied by your network.

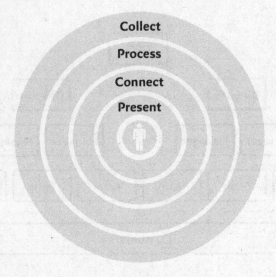

There are four primary rings:

Present: The presentation ring collates the outputs of the other rings and presents them to the customer in a common language to minimize the friction in any interactions. The presentation ring is also where information flows from the customer into the organization.

Connect: The connection ring bridges the process and presentation rings and ensures consistency of data between the different process segments. In real-world terms this is typically your data infrastructure, but it also represents the management processes and interactions that ensure efficient communication.

Process: The process ring is where the meat of the business happens. It represents all of the core business functions (product development, manufacturing, finance, HR) or departments that are necessarily abstracted away from the relationship with the customer. Note that if we are pushing power towards the edge of the organization (see Part 3), and much of that is towards the customer, some of these functions may span into the presentation ring. In other words, some functions that you might currently attribute to the back office should perhaps be conducted by the people or systems that are serving customers directly.

Collect: This is where the organization interfaces with the physical world and other organizations. It is primarily an inbound interface for services and products, such as the supply chain.

Let us start at the heart of the diagram. Why do we place the customer at the centre?

Customer centricity

Lots of companies describe themselves as 'customer-centric'. This is to differentiate them from companies that might be 'product-centric'. Product-centric organizations are seen as exhibiting something of a legacy mindset, whereby a company would be founded on an innovative idea and then be built around seeking a receptive audience for that product. Product-centric companies are seen to be led by what is possible, and often what excites the designer of the product, more than what the customer might actually want.

Many companies, one of my own past endeavours included, are founded on what seems like a powerful idea but then struggle to find a market to appreciate it. This is why you hear so much in the start-up media about 'product market fit', and 'pivoting'. Pivots come when founders accept that their bright idea doesn't map to a profitable audience and they decide to pursue a different avenue.

On the flip side, as the apocryphal Henry Ford quote goes, 'If we had asked the customer what they wanted, they would have asked for a faster horse.' Customer-centric companies are at risk of producing less innovation if all their development is led by the customer. How will they make the great leaps driven by moments of insight if all they do is make iterative improvements based on customer feedback?

The reality is that all established businesses must operate with a balance of customer-centricity and product-centric innovation that takes leaps beyond what the customer can imagine. But for day-to-day operational success with the minimum amount of friction, the customer must be at the heart of what the company does. Not least because in this age of low friction, competition is so constant, fierce and fast-evolving. Your connection to the customer and the trust that engenders may be the only things that differentiate you from your peers at various points in the market cycle. That customer connection can sustain you through those periods when the competition steals ahead. It can be a source of critical competitive insight that allows you to respond with your own iterative innovations more quickly.

Assembling your customer-facing ring properly can also strip much friction from the internal operations of the organization, freeing time for bigger leaps forward in strategic and product thinking.

So, what does this ring look like?

Presentation ring

In the presentation ring, the aim is to eliminate inconsistency in the language, tone, design, culture and data used in the interaction with customers.

Inconsistency in these factors is a significant source of friction in the relationship with customers and causes expensive knock-on effects inside the organization. A 2014 study by global management consulting company McKinsey found that customer satisfaction across the whole user journey is 30 per cent more predictive of their overall happiness as a customer than any single interaction. More importantly, the study found that a consistent customer journey has the power to lower the cost of serving customers by as much as 20 per cent.[7] As Jake Sorofman, vice president of IT service management at Gartner, puts it: 'In the game of customer experience, I'd argue that consistency will always trump delight.'[8]

Think about the growing diversity of customer touch points that you have now and you can see the rising challenge of ensuring a consistent experience. How do you speak a consistent language across advertising, media coverage, social media, word of mouth, conference presentations, trade show stands, sales literature, partner literature, telesales, point of sale, ecommerce listings, website and more? These touch points all come before you have even converted the prospect into a customer. This is why every touch point that the customer has with you must be considered as part of a ring and every function in that ring must be operating to the same standards.

Each functional unit in this ring must subscribe to the same standards across the following areas:

Design

This has become a critical part of the toolkit for maximizing the conversion rate of customers and minimizing the friction involved in self-service. Design also has an enormous role to play in accessibility, overcoming issues of disability or language. Get the design right and you can demolish barriers to sales and reduce the cost of servicing customers, as well as increasing their loyalty. In research I did with Salesforce in 2016, we asked ecommerce customers about the factors that drove their loyalty. We didn't mention design specifically, but all the highest-ranking factors after price were about reducing friction: easy payment options, fast delivery, having the right stock on hand. These expectations are highly portable: what we build up in our consumer lives seems to translate strongly into our behaviours in a business context.

Language

As organizations grow organically and functions move further apart, their language tends to drift – just as it does in countries or continents, creating local accents or dialects. This can be confusing for customers and creates barriers to internal communication. One frequent and simple example is in databases. Often, when clients have been going through digital transformation programmes, they find multiple internal databases storing the same information but under different field headings, making consolidation and interoperation so much harder. Across rings the language used to describe products and services, down to every field on a form a customer is asked to complete, must be consistent.

Tone

Clearly, tone needs some variation across the business: you don't speak to customers the same way when chasing bad debts as you do when trying to attract them in the first place. But there should be a coherence in the corporate personality that doesn't jar across interactions. This feeds into design, training, call-centre scripts, sales behaviour and other parts of the business. It is a critical extension of the brand.

Which functions exist in the presentation ring? You might be surprised to find that elements of five or more different departments exist in this ring. And from each of those departments there may be many different functions, depending on the level to which you have broken these functions down. It reduces to this: who has direct interaction with the customer?

- **Sales:** telesales, field sales, pre-sales consultancy, account management.
- **Marketing:** telemarketing, email campaigns, web, social media, PR/media relations, design.
- **Operations:** logistics/delivery, returns, third-party courier services.
- **Support:** customer services, technical support.
- **Finance:** order to cash, debt management.

Bear in mind the power that all these functions have over your sustained relationship with the customer, particularly if you are pursuing the model of pushing power to the edge of the organization, as suggested in Part 3. In each of these functions, people may be taking the initiative. If they are, you want them to do so in a manner that is commensurate with the other functions of the ring. Thinking about all these processes as part of one coherent whole helps to shape the rules and boundaries you place around those people at the edge of the organization.

Connection ring

In around 2013 I spoke to a client who was belatedly embarking on a digital transformation programme. They told me they had forty-seven different 'core' software platforms on which the organization operated. These were not forty-seven computer programs or mobile apps, like Microsoft Office; this was forty-seven different, dedicated software platforms for different lines of business and functions in the organization. Each software platform fitted essentially the same template. There was a database crammed with information about customers, services or finances. On top of that database was a series of different interfaces to allow different workers in the organization to interact with the data.

At the time I thought this was absurd. To have much of the same data replicated so many times, with all the inefficiency, risk and threat of poor customer service that this presents. But I have since learned that this organization was operating on relatively consolidated systems. I have met others with forty-seven different systems *just* for billing their customers. I have met organizations whose leaders have lost count of the total number of software platforms as it approached four figures.

The connection ring represents the consolidation of these systems. There are no business functions that sit here, as such, but rather business systems. You may, however, choose to site the functions responsible for managing these systems notionally in this layer.

At the most basic level, the connection layer requires a consistent data model, so that everyone is dealing with data using the same terms. The ultimate example might be a single server containing all the company's data, though this is not always possible or even desirable for various reasons. It can be excessively expensive to the point where the business case does not justify it. And there can be arguments around privacy and data security for segmenting corporate data into different systems.

The right approach is to start with the objective – or, more likely, objectives. What are the benefits of building coherence in the connection ring? These might include:

- **Reducing internal friction:** Consolidating or at least connecting data reduces the number of times that they must be re-entered, cutting down on administrative costs and speeding internal processes.
- **Reducing external friction:** Cleaner data models can drive quicker and more accurate customer service.
- **Minimizing risk:** There are enormous risks inherent in inaccurate data and particularly in constant re-entry, as highlighted by the example below.
- **Transparency and analysis:** A single, shared data model enables much greater transparency through the organization, giving far more insight in support of strategic and operational decisions.

In the last few years, many companies have taken the plunge to completely rebuild their data store into a single 'data lake' or 'data warehouse'. This might satisfy the neat freak in us, but it often isn't necessary, if systems can be made to talk to each other. Trying to interconnect forty-seven fundamentally similar systems might be a waste of effort. Clearly, some consolidation is required. But when you have a handful of systems, as long as they are reasonably modern, they can usually be made to communicate and share data effectively. Even for older systems, robotic process automation (RPA) platforms can usually find clever ways to act as a go-between for them. For example, some of these systems can plug in to a keyboard and monitor port and act as a virtual human, shuttling data between systems in very manual fashion.

Before you invest in a forklift upgrade, start with the general guidelines above and make them specific. For example, one client of mine in procurement had a serious compound incident with data re-entry. Someone had missed a zero off a pack size in the database. The database said that each pack contained ten units of the item in question. In fact, it contained a hundred units. Then someone else misunderstood an order that came in – again by a factor of ten. Instead of ordering one box of ten units, they ordered ten boxes. Now, to satisfy an order of ten units, they had 1,000. And for this item, ten units was an unusually large order. Years after this had happened, they still had hundreds of the item in the warehouse.

This was a great example of the risk inherent in their manual systems for order processing that required repeated data re-entry. And it was the basis of the business case that drove them to invest in better systems.

Process ring

The process ring is where any back-office functions that do not belong in proximity to the customer sit, as well as operational management. Note that in many ways your strategic management sits outside of the ring model, abstracted to the point where you can have clear oversight of what happens day-to-day.

Examples of functions that sit here include:

- **Finance:** budgeting, forecasting, reporting, payroll.
- **HR:** recruitment, development, benefits.
- **Operations:** manufacturing, warehousing, stock control.
- **Product:** R&D, new product development (though this likely involves interactions with customers so could sit across the two rings).

The process ring contains a mixture of functions that will be highly specialized and unique to your organization, and highly generic functions that could exist inside or outside the walls of the business. Here again, coherence is critical, but in the process ring it is about the coherence of objectives and culture.

Collection ring

The collection ring is where your operations interface with suppliers up- and downstream in the value chain. Where this boundary sits is somewhat up to you: in a networked business, why should you consider the most distant retailer three steps down the value chain any less a part of your organization? But for sanity's sake, we need to define limits somewhere and the collection ring is it.

Key functions in this ring might include any upstream or downstream logistics, procurement, accounts payable, etc.

Here again, consistency is absolutely critical. One of the

success factors for a networked business is minimizing the friction at the interface points between each node in the network. The collection ring is likely to house some of your most critical interactions and it is also likely to be a place where you have a growing number of interactions as the business environment becomes more complex and diverse. So, to minimize friction you need to invest in these interfaces.

Increasingly, this means ensuring that people can work with you in the most digital fashion possible: via some form of API or other electronic data interchange.

Gaps in your model

Even if you have completed a full set of unit templates for your entire business, and have assembled them neatly into the ring model, you will likely find gaps. There will be gaps in understanding, gaps in the 'glue' that joins units together, and often gaps inside the capabilities of the units and their staff.

Key gaps to look for include:

Does your technology infrastructure support low-friction interaction between units? A great way to see this is to look at the amount of email traffic or phone conversations between units. In some places I have even identified issues by looking at the number of people travelling between floors in a building to go and talk to colleagues in other lines of business.

Does the culture of the business encourage entrepreneurial leadership in the units? Look for the levels of collaboration between internal functions, not on operational issues but strategic ones: is the finance team offering number-crunching capabilities to the marketing team, for example? Are any functional units sharing their services with other customers, either inside the group or beyond?

Do you have the personnel to take ownership of each unit and operate them on a semi-autonomous basis? Do you have thought-leaders in junior leadership positions who are active in their industry bodies or on particular issues? This is a good marker of people who are ready to go beyond their current role.

More likely you will be adding units one at a time, working each through the model. As you do, you will find new questions emerging. Is the unit competitive when benchmarked against external providers? If not, do the added benefits of integration outweigh the costs? Remember that outsourcing is often not as low friction in practice as it is in theory, so unless there are improvements in internal interactions first this is not a straightforward alternative.

Even if you do not use this model as a basis for rethinking the structure of the business, I have found it has great value as an analytical tool, laying bare gaps in your knowledge, exposing missing metrics and identifying high-friction points in the workflow of your business.

Human touch

In describing both the functional models and the rings, I have talked a lot about technology, particularly at the interface points. But I've talked very little about human-to-human communication. You might even believe I think people need to stop talking at work. But, in reality, quite the opposite is true.

Amazon – 'Work hard. Have fun. Make conversation'

Amazon is one of the most networked and least monolithic organizations in the world. Ever since CEO Jeff Bezos circulated on infamous memo in 2004, the business has been divided into functional blocks wrapped in software. This allows the leadership to experiment very cost effectively with new ideas and extend the brand into new areas. And that allows the units themselves to be highly entrepreneurial: witness the success of Amazon Web Services, one of the world's largest cloud hosting companies and responsible at the last count for 80 per cent of Amazon's profits.

The interactions between Amazon's functions may be powered by software but clearly even Bezos, the famous micromanager doesn't want to stop people talking altogether. Automating and streamlining your day-to-day interactions makes time for the more important, more human aspects of business. Inside the organization that means strategy, innovation and creativity; for personal development, coaching and leadership.

At the edges of the organization, we need to eliminate the 'bad friction' in our customer and partner relationships. The friction that costs time, money and patience. This makes time for what I call 'good friction'. Good friction is the arm around the customer's shoulder. It is the reassurance, the consultancy, the relationship-building. It is the moments that build loyalty that goes beyond price and efficient service.

We can only make time for this good friction if we invest in eliminating the bad. And a lot of our in-work communication is based on bad friction: people using personal skills to overcome poor processes and systems.

1.5   Models and Reality

Stratification is a model, and as I acknowledged at the start of this section, models do not always map perfectly to reality. There is always an element of adjustment and compromise, even to the theories underpinning the model. For example, how do you square the investment in automation and accelerated information with focusing on agility rather than optimization? Surely those investments are the definition of optimization? Here is where the binary choice between optimization and agility starts to become more nuanced.

Ambidextrous leadership

Stratification is all about building an organization for extreme adaptability. At the start of this section I posited this as an absolute choice: you can be optimized or you can be agile but not both. But obviously we cannot stop improving our processes and always focus on what's next. Some continuing improvement is still required. BMW's approach is an acknowledgement of this duality.

BMW and ambidextrous leadership

One concept you will hear mentioned by leaders inside BMW's UK operations is that of 'ambidextrous leadership'. This is the idea of maintaining focus on two clear sets of seemingly contradictory objectives: how do we continue to improve on what we do today? And how do we adapt and iterate our planning and build for tomorrow's uncertain and ever-changing world?

This concept is being embedded in leaders across the business through the latest iteration of the company's Leadership Development Programme, run in partnership with the consultancy Strategic Leadership.

'For many years now, our business success has been built on continuous improvement. We have strived to deliver operational excellence in all that we do. Today we know that is not enough on its own. While recognizing the importance of maintaining process stability and consistency, we also have to embed in our leaders a greater focus on adaptability and experimentation. This is our ambidextrous leadership challenge,' said Wayne Morse, Leadership Development and Change Management, BMW (UK) Manufacturing Ltd.

Chris Atkinson, UK Managing Director of Strategic Leadership, adds, 'More and more, the companies that we work with are recognizing that strategic leadership is about more than optimization. They are seeking to build skills of entrepreneurship, creativity and innovation across the organization to help them prepare for what comes next.'

There is an interesting interaction between this concept and stratification. Ambidextrous leadership is about how you balance the challenges of today and the opportunities of tomorrow. It is about how you deliver operational excellence, while at the same time exploring the horizon for future growth. In the language I use most often, it is about how you balance optimization with adaptation.

In the stratification model, each functional segment fulfils a specific role. The leadership of the functional unit can try to optimize for that unit's narrow purpose. But critically, that purpose can be abstracted from its role in the wider business. For example, if you have a unit that is fantastic at milling aluminium, it doesn't have to consider itself as only the aluminium milling unit of the company. Its leadership can be entrepreneurial. They can look for opportunities to make aluminium parts for other customers. Some of these new customers might be inside the business but many will be external. This is a low level of ambidextrous leadership.

High-level ambidexterity comes from the leadership who have oversight of all the rings and functions. Once the organization is divided into functional units, leaders have a box of building blocks to play with. They can reassemble the blocks to meet new challenges. They can create new blocks without affecting the other functions. They can use blocks from other people's organizations easily. Or, in the worst cases, they can shut blocks down.

This approach allows the lower-level functions to keep the priority of delivering operational excellence, something they are well drilled in and something that is often critical to the continued success of the wider organization. Where they are stretched to think about future opportunities, it is within a narrow context of their known abilities.

Meanwhile, the senior leadership can take a more long-term, holistic view. They should be freed, both in time and responsibility, from the day-to-day operations of the lower-level units, each of which should have its own effective and entrepreneurial leader. This is what we will explore in more detail in Part 3.

Structuring your future-proof business at a glance

Here is a distillation of Part 1, the critical takeaways to remember when future-proofing the structure of your business:

- In an age of high-frequency change, adaptability is more important than optimization in determining long-term, sustainable success.
- Networks of building bricks provide an agile model for future-proof businesses.
- Networks depend on strong interfaces. Ensure that every function in your network has a low-friction interface to the other functions with which it communicates.

Part 2 How to See the Future

It has never been more important for leaders to look to the future. Yet few find the time to do so, and when they do, they are unsure where to begin.

In this section I share some simple tools for looking to both near and far horizons. These will enable you to define more clearly a direction for your business and help you to identify any obstacles you might meet along the way.

2.1 The Three Horizons

Since there have been companies, their leaders have looked to the future. What is a company, in fact, but a bet on customers' future needs? The ability to predict trends is a vital skill for any leader in business, at whatever level they work, and one that has growing value, but 'foresight', 'horizon scanning' or just plain old 'planning', whatever you want to call it, is something rarely taught and often poorly exercised.

In Part 1 we learned how to build a framework for an agile, future-proof organization. In Part 2 we shall explore some of the techniques that you can employ as a leader to decode the clues that foreshadow forthcoming trends in your industry and build them into your day-to-day activities.

Why do we look to the future?

The future has a habit of sneaking up on us. If we leave decisions and actions until the last moment, it is often too late to do what needs to be done. The time to shop for a dinner party is not when the guests arrive. So, we plan and act in advance.

The way we think about the future, and the types of preparatory actions we can take, are very much affected by how far ahead we are looking. For example, imagine you have an important meeting in the morning. You can, with a reasonable degree of certainty, plan an outfit, work out your route to the meeting, and even prepare what you will say when you get in there. You are operating in a known system with a familiar set of parameters. Your plan might still be disrupted by heavy traffic or a late train, the person you are scheduled to meet could cancel or your child suddenly fall ill. But these are recognizable variables.

Now recall an occasion when you have tried to plan further out. Think about your first answers to that classic childhood question, 'What do you want to be when you grow up?' Most of us who answered 'doctor', 'astronaut', 'prime minister' or 'train driver' will not have ended up in those roles. We were planning with very little understanding of the system in which our career might operate, or the changes that might happen along the way. We were just laying out what, to our naïve minds, was an ideal state at some distant point in the future.

Even as adults, planning decades ahead is challenging. Over the course of those decades, much may change. It is impossible for us to hold all the variables in our heads that might define reality by the time we reach the forecast period. But thinking about the far future is nonetheless a valuable exercise: we may have got the detail of our careers wrong, but at least we staked out an ambition to succeed.

The same modes of thinking about the future, near and far, are important in a business context. We need to look to the near future, where change is largely defined by a group of actors and events that we can understand, even if we cannot predict those events with absolute certainty, and we need to look to the more distant future, laying out long-term goals, and a mission for the business to achieve, accepting that the way we reach it may be as different from today's expectation as our current careers are from that dream of being an astronaut.

Why DON'T we look to the future?

Given the importance of defining our objectives, and looking out for the pitfalls that might prevent us from reaching them, it seems obvious that every leader should spend lots of time looking to the future. And yet I have never met a leader who feels they are able to devote sufficient time to this mode of thinking. Instead, they are consumed by the here and now.

Many things prevent us from looking to the future. It is the classic leader's challenge of working *on* the business versus working *in* the business. There is always a fire to fight, results to deliver, or someone knocking on your door with a question. So, we find it hard to carve out the time to step back and look up.

There are practical things we can do to make time. Delegation is one. Automation is another. Both of these are covered in Part 3. But ultimately it is a question of priorities. We have to recognize the importance of looking to the future for the sake of our business. Leadership is about making time to think beyond the here and now.

Can we see the future?

There is a set of forces that are perhaps not immutable, but that are, at the very least, slow to change. These forces drive us in particular directions. Some of these forces spring from human nature, some from the fundamentals of the capitalist economic system. If you understand properly where we are today, and how these forces drive us, then like a sailor plotting a course driven by the prevailing winds, when predicting the future you can make a pretty good guess where we might end up.

This rather Newtonian approach does not work for everything. It is much better at the macro than the micro. And it is much better at helping you to see *what* might happen, rather than *when* it might happen.

We can see this when we look back at the predictions of the past – ones at which we frequently laugh. What I often find is that what the predictor got wrong was not the destination but the journey time. The paperless office? It's coming, but slowly. Office paper sales are dropping about 2 per cent a year.[1] We probably won't be totally paperless (or near enough so as not to count) for at least a decade or two yet. But we will get there.

What about flying cars? Just a couple of years ago we were still laughing about century-old predictions that we would have flying cars by now. Yet we have recently seen multiple companies launch practical designs. There will soon be commercial flying taxi services, running giant drones with pods for humans between cities and airports in various countries around the world.

Could we have had flying cars before now? Or the paperless office? Yes, if we had improved certain technologies more and adopted them faster. Invested in them more. But the speed at which we make the relevant research leaps, development investments, policy shifts and cultural adaptations to certain changes is deeply unpredictable because they exist in the realm of human collective behaviour and are subject to a multitude of conflicting forces. To come back to my ship analogy, we can see the start and end points of our voyage, and plot a rough path, but we will always encounter a storm at some point along the way. It is impossible to say with certainty how long the ship will be delayed by that storm. It might even sink.

Thus, the visions of the future we produce, by whatever method, are really probabilities rather than predictions. Our response to them has to be measured as such. The nearer the impact looks and the more it is based on observable trends and identifiable issues, the greater the certainty with which we can act on what we see. Indeed, the faster we will need to act in order to maximize the opportunity or avoid the threat. As we look further out, we need to take a more balanced approach, judging our investment in responses against the certainty in what we have seen.

What is clear is that investing even modest amounts in looking to the future provides us with an advantage. Because, as I will go on to show, most organizations, including your competitors, do it very poorly. I recommend to all my clients that leaders at all levels should be incentivized to spend 1 per cent of their time looking to the future. That is roughly just one full working day every six months. Can you find that much time to think about the future of your business? I hope so.

We have talked about the far future, the place of our goals and ambitions. And the near future, the place of plans and actions. If we were to break that near-term future down further, we might separate the year ahead from the years beyond that. In the immediate future, we must ensure that we have the cash, materials and resources to continue doing business. We must make sure that our people are properly organized to deliver against expectations. We budget, and plan, typically with the goal of improving or optimizing business performance: delivering more revenue – and, ideally, profit – with lower costs.

Further out, but still in the near term, we must look at how the business might change. Or at least we should. As I will show, this is the time period that is least well examined in business. This range takes us out to perhaps the next decade at most.

Beyond this, all certainty starts to drift away and we are

beginning to think about a very different world. But it is still an important process. Thinking about the far future is how we define what we want our business to be, its mission and its purpose beyond the next year's profits.

These three different modes of thinking about the future can be usefully divided into what are known as the Three Horizons.

Three Horizons model

The Three Horizons model[2] was developed in 2000 by the global consultancy McKinsey. Then, it was a means of helping company leaders to think about growth. Today, following the work of the International Futures Forum, it is much more widely applied to societal-scale challenges, as well as internal company exercises.

The Three Horizons framework asks us to visualize the future in three different sections (see diagram).

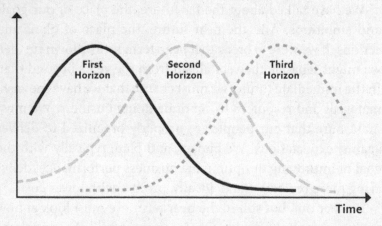

The first horizon

The first horizon represents today and the immediate future. In theory, this is business as usual. In my analogies, you are planning your outfit for the day ahead. In the McKinsey model, the first horizon is the one in which you focus on optimizing today's business model. How can you extract maximum value from the business activities that you currently undertake?

Historically, we might have considered the next two to three years (or more) to be a stable period in which our business would continue to operate using known parameters with the usual challenges of competition and cash flow. I will go on to show that we perhaps must think a little differently today.

The third horizon

Skipping the second horizon for a moment, let us look to the far future, however far out you determine that to be. This is a much less certain place. It is a place of hopes and dreams, fears and expectations. In traditional foresight exercises we would use the third horizon as a canvas onto which we would project our ideal scenarios. What is your vision for the business? How might the business model and proposition change? Who will be the customers and how will they buy?

Creating the platform for a reasonable discussion about the third horizon is in many ways the value of the Three Horizons framework. It allows us, even forces us, to leave the issues of the here and now behind and focus on what lies beyond. Today's travails can be firmly placed in horizon one and we can open ourselves up to thinking about a future that might be very different. We explore different scenarios that might play out depending on the prevailing trends in the economy, society, technology and the environment.

In the McKinsey model, the third horizon is about the realization of today's 'moon shot' attempts, the relatively risky ventures and experiments that you might invest in today for disruptive growth in the future. Where McKinsey's model and broader, societal-scale foresight exercises diverge is in how far out the third horizon might sit. In major foresight exercises, the third horizon might typically sit at twenty to thirty years. In McKinsey's growth model it might only be five to seven years.

The second horizon

Now we come to the period in between: the second horizon. In broader foresight models, the second horizon is where the action happens. Having defined where we are today, and where we want to be, the second horizon is where we take the actions that will move us from A to B. By looking at the gap between the reality (first horizon) and the vision (third horizon) we can define the steps we need to take in order to make the vision real.

In the original McKinsey model, the second horizon is rather more limited. It is about how we move today's business model on with iteration and innovation. How you can extend the product line or expand into new categories, developing the model to grow and sustain its viability.

When you are thinking about the second horizon for your business, you are really looking at the next one to three years. In the past, this second horizon may have been further out. But the nature of high-frequency change means that every business continually needs to be evolving its proposition, if not preparing the next.

Where it all falls down

It is a useful rule of thumb that most people will lose their sense of perspective about the future of the business after just six months being inside it. Six months working in a company or industry is enough, in my experience, to condition people to believe that the way the business works today is the way it will always work. That the rules of the sector it operates in are largely immutable.

You know people have lost perspective when they respond to new ideas with a flat: 'That won't work here,' or look at innovations from outside and say: 'But this industry is different.' If you hear these phrases from colleagues when introducing new ideas, you know you may have a challenge on your hands.

When trying to get people to think about the future, the big challenge has therefore always been to break people out of this blinkered view. The Three Horizons model has been very valuable for that. In fact, both the McKinsey model and the more extended versions have been used with great success to get people to leave their current expectations in the here and now, and think with more open minds about the future.

The problem comes with the timescales. Considering the distant third horizon always used to be the greatest challenge. Now, in the age of high-frequency change, it may be the greatest distraction.

Very few organizations have any formalized capability for radical adaptation to threats that appear on the near horizon – the second horizon or even the first, in the Three Horizons model. Corporate planning is based explicitly on a business-as-usual model because everyone is focused on trying to meet near-term performance goals. This leaves very little time to think beyond the next quarter or year.

This creates a problem with Three Horizons foresight exercises. Here, people are encouraged to leave behind the realities of today and consider the third horizon, a distant, very different future. The result is that even today's perceived threats can be shunted into that distant horizon, a problem for tomorrow, not today. Potential responses then get treated as issues for the second horizon, leaving years for these actions to be completed.

In an age of high-frequency change, that is often too late.

Shifting assumptions

The impact of high-frequency change is not just to produce disruption on the first and second horizons, but to shift the assumptions that can be made when considering the third.

Take an example of high-frequency change that has made a lot of relatively recent science fiction already seem dated: vaping. The combination of low-friction global supply chains, rapid Chinese manufacturing innovation and shared online culture made vape shops a feature on every suburban high street in just a couple of years, starting in around 2012. If the current trend continues, health scares notwithstanding, vaping will largely replace smoking.

Just a few years ago, science fiction writers like Richard Morgan, author of *Altered Carbon*, were envisioning scenarios in which characters still smoked traditional cigarettes in the 2300s. This now seems like an anachronism.

Thinking near and far

What does high-frequency change mean for future-proofing our business? It means we must keep a watchful eye on the near and far horizons, and understand the different value in each exercise.

Think of your organization as a nomadic tribe. The tribe is always seeking better land on which to settle for a while. Every few years the tribal elders get together and discuss what would be the ideal locality. What is the relative importance of water, coastline, fertile earth, wild animals and forest? They weigh the options and set the direction towards where they believe they will find the optimum environment that will deliver the greatest returns for the tribe. They consider too what obstacles they might find along the way.

This is your long-distance foresight. It is full of uncertainties and driven by ideals. But it is critical because it is how you orient the business towards the future.

Now consider the journey itself. Along the way the tribe's forward scouts will constantly encounter new obstacles and opportunities. Unknown oases and marauding bandits, potential trading partners, difficult terrain. The tribal leaders must rapidly reroute or take decisions as to how to respond to each opportunity before the situation is upon them.

This is your near-distance foresight. It is predicated on visible threats and opportunities, and deals with real and near-immediate action.

Each of these time frames requires a different approach to foresight. Two tools will be outlined in section 2.3 but first, we should look at the foresight and strategy exercises you already do today.

2.2 Why Your Future-proofing Strategies Aren't Working

Before we look at the tools that you might use to look to the future, it's worth examining the tools that you already use today, and why they may not be fit for purpose. While all companies plan, few do it truly effectively. Let's start with the simplest (in theory) and most common form of planning: the annual budget.

Budget and strategy

Every year you lay out the company's expected performance for the year ahead. Or perhaps the finance director or CFO does. This process is usually collaborative or, in the worst cases, combative. It requires input from every line of business and function. How much will the sales team commit to bringing in? What will the marketing team spend to help sales achieve that goal? How many people does HR expect to bring on board to support these initiatives?

The resulting document is often quite complex, especially if it is being produced on a spreadsheet, as so many still are. The combination of complexity and collaboration can mean it takes a very long time for a budget to be produced and signed off. To shorten this period, each year's budget usually starts with last year's. The spreadsheet (or more likely, collection of interlinked spreadsheets) is opened up, saved under a new name, and the process starts again.

Alongside this process there is usually a strategy-setting exercise led by the MD or CEO. It would be nice to think that this was an open-minded assessment of the future. In my experience, having read many of these documents, the strategy can usually be summed up as 'bigger, better, faster, more' with a sprinkling of 'nicer, kinder, greener' over the top. Annual strategy documents are rarely based on the understanding that radical change might be required. With few exceptions, they are plans for optimizing today's business, not adapting to a foreseen new reality.

In an ideal world the strategy-setting exercise precedes the budgeting process. After all, you want to make sure that any strategic priorities have appropriate levels of budget allocated to them. Unfortunately, because the budgeting process takes so long, and the strategy-setting process is often compressed by the realities of day-to-day management, the two frequently happen in parallel.

The result, according to some research I carried out with the Canadian financial software company Prophix, is that two-thirds of CFOs say that the budget is at best connected to the strategy at a high level. For many, there is little or no relationship between the two.

In short, in the most frequent foresight exercises conducted by companies, there is little assessment of the world beyond the boundaries of the company and the state of the sector in which it operates. And what strategy is set is poorly supported by investment.

Strategic response – medium term

Occasionally a more radical plan is put into place. In most cases, though, this tends to be a reactive rather than proactive exercise. It is usually triggered by issues that are already causing material harm to the business, rather than trends that were spotted early through formal horizon scanning.

The tone of the response to these situations is rarely a positive one. Forced to respond at speed, the company brings in external resources from a consultant – usually Accenture or one of the big four if the company is sufficiently large.[3] Words like 'repositioning', 'rightsizing' and 'restructuring' abound. Or, more recently, 'remodelling'.

If 80 per cent of the responses to these colossal issues crashing into the business is to cut and retreat, the other 20 per cent is almost as scary. The minority of cases involve the big bet, the rapid expenditure of cash in the pursuit of growth or the competitors who have streaked ahead with some new innovation. The question to be answered is 'How can we do what they do?' but without the five years of planning and development that 'they' put into it. It is a cash-fuelled shortcut and it often fails. Take the wave of 'digital transformation' undertaken by large enterprises over the last two decades as established companies tried to catch up with their digitally native challengers. The reported failure rate for corporate transformations was first estimated at 70 per cent in 1996 by John Kotter in his book *Leading Change*.[4] McKinsey's 2018 global survey on transformation put the failure rate at 74 per cent.[5] This included big digital transformation programmes at global leaders like Ford, GE and Procter & Gamble.[6] The failures weren't fatal, but they cost each business time, money and goodwill, delaying their attempts to catch up or overtake the competition.

Five-year planning

Real, strategic planning exercises tend to be infrequent. Periodically, the leadership decides that it has been a while since they got a real chance to work not *in* the business, but *on* it. So, they ask their assistants to schedule an away day with the leadership team. This usually takes place, in my experience, in a venue that has close connections with the most senior leader's hobby. That might be an excellent golf course, or maybe some good cycling routes these days, as cycling seems to be the new executive pastime of choice.

A room is booked, everyone is invited to dress down and a moderator is brought in to run the day. The process usually involves Post-it notes and lots of invocations to think 'blue-sky' or 'out of the box'. After a few hours of curling sandwiches and bad coffee, everyone adjourns to the bar and one person is tasked with translating the output of the day – variable in quality, specificity and direction – into a long-term strategy or five-year plan.

The next day, hungover from one too many single-malt whiskies shared at the hotel bar, the team heads out onto the golf course.

I poke fun, but I don't mean to imply these exercises are not important. They provide a rare opportunity for people to look upwards and outwards. They can be a great bonding opportunity for the team. But they are riddled with problems:

- The sessions are infrequent.
- Those in the room rarely come from diverse backgrounds or hold diverse opinions.

- The strategy that results often lacks clarity and direction . . .
- . . . and it is very often ignored once everyone returns to business as usual.

Naturally, the premises on which the new strategy was based become rapidly outdated, further reinforcing everyone's opinion that they just need to knuckle down and work harder at what they were already doing. Business as usual persists until the company accelerates into a wall of customer apathy.

Need for change

Running a business based on the current array of budgeting, strategy and response processes is a recipe for disaster. Combine this with the near-exclusive focus on process optimization (see Part 1), and you have a recipe for a company that will, sooner or later, drive itself into a dead end, blind to the changing world in which it is operating. This is not the type of company any of us wants to run and it is not the fate of a company for which any of us wants to be responsible.

I will let you into a secret: I have a soft spot for established businesses over start-ups. Start-ups get all the love and attention for being cool and different, for innovating and breaking rules. But for all the occasional pieces of corporate misbehaviour, established organizations are often better employers and better corporate citizens. A behemoth being brought down and replaced with the ravaging wolves of the start-up scene is not always to be celebrated as progress, part of Schumpeter's inevitable wind of creative destruction.[7] If we can equip established businesses to be their own disruptors, to see change coming and adapt to the new world, we need never face the inefficiency and distress caused by company collapse.

The first step to avoiding this fate is to change the way your company looks at the future, from the most basic budgeting to proper foresight exercises and long-term visioning. In fact, investing in your current budgeting and strategy-setting processes with technology and training is a fantastic way to free up time for more open-minded foresight activity.

2.3 Scanning the Far Horizon

Now let's look at some of the more effective ways to look to the future and plan ahead. Taking your Three Horizons model, start with the furthest, the third horizon, which will look ten years ahead or more.

Scenario planning

Scenario planning is exactly what it sounds like: a process of creating multiple scenarios in order to understand how you might plan for them. When scanning the far future, scenario planning is a useful tool.

There are many variants of the scenario-planning process that range from the simple to the highly complex. At its simplest, scenario planning is storytelling. It started at the RAND Corporation, where Herman Kahn used to tell stories to help people understand the different ways hostile states might use nuclear weapons.

At its most complex, scenario planning integrates systems thinking (literally, analysing all the components in a system to understand how all those factors interact) and deep empirical analysis (research). The final stages of the process are usually the same, though:

1 Create a series of stories about possible versions of the future.

2 Tell these stories to a group of people, ideally from diverse perspectives – you need people from inside and outside the business and from a variety of backgrounds, ages, sexes, ethnicities and more.

3 Ask your participants to think about how they would respond in the scenarios described in each story.

4 Work back from those responses to understand the implications for today's strategy.

The implications for today's strategy might mean steps you can take to mitigate the worst outcomes. Or investments you can make to give you the best chance of realizing future opportunities, should they present themselves.

So, how do you create the stories in the first place? The starting point should always be to identify the critical drivers of success for your business. What are the biggest factors that will determine your future growth and profitability? Is it the macro-economic environment? Is it regulation? Is it the price of raw materials? In scenario-planning sessions I have led or participated in, we have used a variety of factors on two axes: authoritarian or libertarian government; more or less environmentalist policy; economic growth vs economic collapse. Whatever factors will have an impact on your business, you can choose.

Of course, you can't address all the factors at once, so you need to do some refining to get it down to two or three key factors. Remember that all foresight processes should be iterative, repeated on a regular schedule. So, you do not have to address everything this time around.

If you can narrow the field down to two critical drivers, then a frequently used method of turning these into scenarios is to plot them on a two-by-two grid. This then gives you four possible scenarios:

- Dimension A low, dimension B low
- Dimension A low, dimension B high
- Dimension A high, dimension B low
- Dimension A high, dimension B high

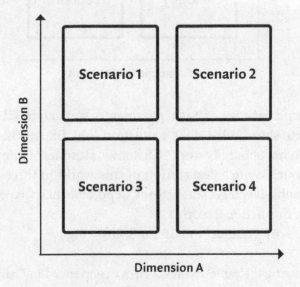

For example, say the two critical factors for success in your business are the macroeconomic environment in the country you operate in and the level of environmental consciousness (and hence regulation) in that country. You plot these on your grid, creating four scenarios that you might title as in the second diagram.

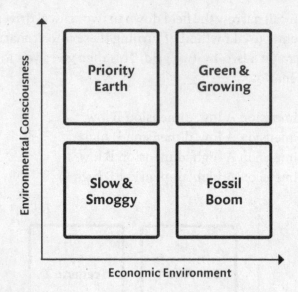

Around each set of basic parameters you can build a more complete story. What does regulation look like in these contexts? What about tax rates? Customer attitudes? Competitive behaviour? Write a description of this world in three or four paragraphs. If you get stuck, think of possible newspaper headlines in this fictional world.

Here's my example for 'Green & Growing':

Following the rapid sea-level rises experienced in California in 2030, the US finally swung its weight behind global climate initiatives and rapidly secured greater harmonization of carbon taxes and other emissions controls. This led to a boom in green infrastructure that has driven rapid growth in the UK, leveraging the country's research base and large renewable resources.

The pictures of the devastation in the US and increasing incidences of flooding and extreme weather in the UK have brought popular opinion in the country in line with the science and poor environmental performers now face harsh criticism from the public and the media.

The speed of transition has brought many challenges to businesses in the UK that were reliant on less clean forms of fuel or raw materials. And the focus of public opprobrium is not always very sophisticated or nuanced. For example, use of palm oil is highly frowned upon, even though alternatives are largely less efficient and more polluting.

Headlines from this world might include:

70% of supermarket products STILL contain 'damaging' palm oil

Budget statement: carbon tax escalator to hit new high

Government agrees pension fund bailout after oil investment collapse

In each scenario, the behaviour of your business is going to be very different, as is its performance. There are two questions for your participants:

- How would you respond in these scenarios?
- What can we do today to minimize the risk or maximize the opportunity should some version of these scenarios arise?

Three-dimensional scenarios

Sometimes you will want to consider more than two drivers in an exercise. And sometimes you might need help building these scenarios and convincing people of their validity. After all, it is quite hard to think yourself into an imaginary scenario ten, twenty or thirty years into the future, whether you are the one writing the scenario or the one listening to someone else's story.

To overcome these issues, I developed a new approach to building scenarios while working alongside a team from across Greater Manchester as they set out to think about the future for the city region's transport infrastructure.

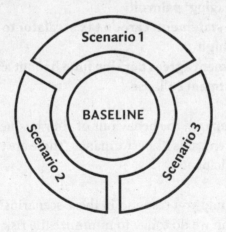

We started with a baseline: what would the world look like in twenty-five years if all the current trends continued on their existing paths? The aim was to create a very plausible scenario that every one of our participants could believe in. Then we took our three primary drivers – the environment, the economy and employment – and 'bent' the baseline scenario in each of those directions to create three new scenarios.

This created three possible futures that were grounded in a reality that, while plausible, was stretched into unexpected places – and so produced unexpected implications. In each of the three new scenarios we imagined how the world would change if society and, by extension, government, prioritized that factor. So, in the environmental scenario we imagined how large-scale decarbonization might play out. In the economic-growth scenario we saw new and existing business hotspots expanding. And in the employment scenario we pictured a more redistributive effect, growing – or restoring – employment to different parts of the city or region.

This approach has a number of benefits:

- It creates a highly plausible baseline that gives your other scenarios credibility with the more sceptical participants.
- It simplifies the storytelling process because you have a baseline to start from and you are focused on only a single driver of change when trying to understand how the new scenario will differ.
- It allows you to develop three or even four scenarios based on different drivers inside a coherent pattern.

The approach also has downsides though:

- All scenario-planning exercises are time-consuming, and building a plausible baseline scenario can be particularly demanding of research time.
- Binding yourself to a 'plausible' baseline scenario can mean that it is harder to imagine more extreme future scenarios. And if the recent past has told us anything, extreme change is always possible.

Scenario planning done right is an inherently time-consuming and expensive process. It is not an exercise you will repeat frequently. Even Shell, the company that is most famous for its use of scenarios, only publishes new scenarios every few years. This creates a sense of fear in people about 'getting it right'. How do you know you have the right drivers or scenarios? Is it a waste of money if you do not?

The answer is to look at the alternative: are you better keeping the blinkers on and not looking to the future? Scenario planning is a narrative, heuristic and inherently qualitative process. It is never going to be precise and it is unlikely ever to be exactly 'right'. But it is the process itself that is important. It unlocks different thinking and builds collaboration. It creates opportunities to examine diverse perspectives. The scenarios themselves are really a vehicle for getting people together to look beyond their traditional boundaries and consider possibilities they haven't before. As *Scientific American* said of Herman Kahn's approach, it is a tool for helping people to 'think the unthinkable'.

What I have outlined here is really only the beginning of scenario planning, a framework with a long history and lots of development by many practitioners. It is just an introduction to get you started. See the sources in the endnotes for more detail, and you will find a wealth of information online.

2.4 The Near Horizon: Opportunities and Risks

A good scenario-planning exercise requires major time commitments from senior people, and days, weeks or even months of prior research. When looking to the near future, or 'the first horizon', I suggest a different approach that can be incorporated into everyday activities within the business.

Intersections

Intersections is a process designed to help you to build a coherent picture of the near future, but also designed to be quicker and cheaper to run than scenario planning, so that it can be run frequently. Intersections is valuable because it is focused on identifying the most immediate issues that present the greatest threat or opportunity to your organization or sector.

The output of this process will form the basis of your strategy for the next year or two. It is designed to be an iterative process. It deliberately throws up a universe of possible outcomes before forcing you to focus only on those that have the greatest and most immediate impact. You do not have to worry about those that you filter out. The process should be run again in six months' time, and then every six months after that. This is the basis of an agile approach to strategy.

Intersections addresses both the internal factors that affect your organization specifically and external factors that affect the whole market.

Macro trends and pressure points

The simple idea behind Intersections is that the greatest changes in your business and industry will happen in places where pressure is *already* building. It says that – even though you may not be able to see them – there are pressure points building in your business today. Change comes when these pressures are exacerbated by the impact of global trends sweeping through your industry. So, we must work to find the intersections between global trends and your specific pressure points before that impact arrives.

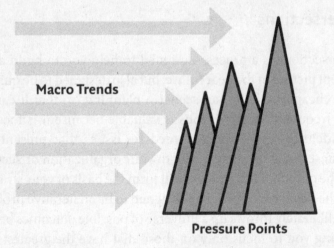

I tend to visualize it as a volley of missiles flying towards a mountain range (see diagram). Some will hit, others will miss. We need to work out which will strike where, and the scale of the resultant impact.

Limiting the scope of your vision

To ensure that Intersections remains a relatively lightweight exercise, and one that can be repeated frequently, we need to cut down the scope of the possibilities. Unlike scenario planning, this is not an exercise for imagining every possibility. It is about uncovering probabilities.

This starts with understanding that Intersections is not about studying *the* future. It is about studying *your* future. Every individual and company has a unique path that will cause them to be affected by different factors at different times. When you run an Intersections exercise you are not trying to imagine the future for the whole world, or even your nearest competitors, though obviously you will share some challenges. You are trying to identify the near-term threats and opportunities that will have the greatest impact on *your* business specifically.

In order to narrow your focus, we must put boundaries on the scope of your vision in three different dimensions: geographical, temporal and technological.

Geography

Change comes at different times to different parts of the world. However global our economy might be, there are still uniquely local cultural, political and economic factors. If your company is global, you need to break down your foresight, region by region, or ideally country by country. Some factors will cross borders; for example, if cyber crime is an issue for your business – and it is of rising importance for most – then it is likely the threat will come from abroad. Likewise, if your analysis identifies threats that are fundamental to your business model, then it is likely that these issues are not specific to your geography. Other issues, such as regulation, resource access, the skills market, financing and political stability, can all be highly dependent on where you are. Given the power of these issues, it makes sense to be highly focused on a single area.

Time

The second dimension in which you are limiting the scope of your vision is time. Intersections is a tool for considering what happens next, in the coming year or two. You are not actively trying to think beyond that, though given the unpredictability of *when* things happen versus *what* happens, you may sometimes identify things that will happen outside of that time frame. One of the first things you learn as a futurist is that it is always much easier to predict what is going to happen than exactly when it will take place.

Technology

The third dimension in which you are limiting the scope of your vision is more of an orientation. It defines how you separate the enormous, global trends that are affecting everyone (the arrows on the left of the diagram), from the points of pressure in your own organization or industry with which those macro trends will intersect (the mountains on the right).

Both the macro trends and the pressure points might fall into a group of headings often described using the acronyms PESTLE (Political, Economic, Scientific, Technological, Legal, Environmental) or STEEP (Scientific, Technological, Environmental, Economic, Political). These are broad headlines to get people thinking about the different sources of influence and drivers of change. They can be very useful in workshops to broaden people's thinking. We all understand the immediate influences on our day-to-day lives at home and work, but sometimes we need pointers to think about those bigger drivers that may be less visible every day but which are nonetheless hugely impactful on our long-term success.

Clearly, all these factors will be important in any horizon-scanning exercise. But the way that Intersections works – looking for the points where one factor intersects with all of the others – means that you need to choose which factors will form the arrows. The others then form the mountains – or at least some of them. You could choose any one of these PESTLE or STEEP factors as the starting point of your macro trends and array the rest of your factors as the pressure points (outlined below). But I always choose a set of technology-driven trends as my starting point.

This is because, of all the PESTLE factors, right now technology is the only one experiencing continuous change at an exponential rate, and whose effects are irreversible. Take the economy, for comparison. During the depths of the recession after 2008, the UK economy shrank by 7 per cent.[8] This was an extremely painful contraction for many, but it was marginal relative to the overall scale of the British economy, and the effect rebounded (albeit slowly) over the following years.

Political instability will be a greater issue in some countries than others. Even in the most challenging economic times, the modern UK is not a country of political revolution. Plot the policies of the major parties on the Political Compass (politicalcompass.org) and you find very little space between them. Even the major shock brought about by the Brexit vote, the subsequent instability in the ruling party and the threats to freedom of movement have had only marginal effects on the day-to-day reality for most people and most businesses. Some people and some companies will be affected dramatically. Nationally, the impact is likely to be significantly negative. But over time those effects are likely to reverse.

The same is true of health shocks. The WHO expects a 'Disease X' pandemic that will be more threatening than SARS. But this too will come and go.

Climate change is a structural change. It will dramatically increase the flood risk in the UK. But, despite dramatic storms, the total costs of disruption are not expected to double for seventy years. In the next two to five years, the time frame we're examining, the change is linear.

Meanwhile, fuelled by military, health and consumer investment, technological development will continue to change at the exponential rate first identified by Intel's Gordon Moore back in the middle of the last century. Moore noted that the number of transistors that could economically be included in a single silicon chip was doubling roughly every two years. This translated into the bang for buck that a computer could deliver doubling every two years. Parallel laws were identified to predict increases in the amount of information that could be stored and the speed at which information could be carried. All were at an exponential rate and all have remained accurate predictors of the rate of change of technology.

Every single company I have worked with for the past seven years has completely accepted that technology simultaneously represents both its greatest threats and its greatest opportunities. This idea has been tested multiple times, including when I had to speak to the UK staff of the German chemicals conglomerate BASF just days after the Brexit referendum. The vote threatened the company with a completely different and much more complicated operating environment, including new trade tariffs and a completely different safety certification regime. Just before I spoke I took Darren Budd, the commercial director, aside and told him what I planned to say: that technology was the greatest driver of change that they faced. He reassured me that their own planning was completely in line with this, even with the outcome of the Brexit vote.

Current affairs often appear to be the most dramatic factors facing company or country. Yet every time I raise the subject with serious, smart leaders they tell me that technological change is still the top of their issue list.

In the geographic space (the UK) and the time frame (one to two years) that you will be addressing with your Intersections exercise, no change driver, however important, will have an effect as powerful and all-encompassing as technology. Rather, changes in technology will fuel change in all other areas. Exactly *how* technology drives change is described in the 'Macro trends' section below.

Pressure points

The Intersections process looks at change impacts that are very specific to your organization. In order to link the big macro trends back to hyper-local effects on your business, you need to look at what I call 'pressure points'. These are issues in your business (internal) or your market (external) that are already presenting as challenges or opportunities. These can take a range of forms: social, financial, operational, technical, legal or regulatory.

Uncovering each group of pressure points requires a different research method, so we will treat the two separately, with two distinct exercises to help you to uncover them.

Internal pressure points
Internal pressure points are the gaps in your armour. They are the failings in your organization around which change is most

likely to come. Finding these internal pressure points is vital for effective near-term futurism, but it is also a useful skill for day-to-day business. If you can identify pressures and propose solutions, you will be highly valued by clients and colleagues.

Typical internal pressure points might include:

- ageing or obsolete infrastructure,
- poor communication between departments,
- slow or difficult internal processes,
- investment in technology,
- internal politics,
- decision-making,
- customer service or reputational issues,
- financial health,
- poor margins,
- space – too much or too little,
- staffing, skills and recruitment.

The way to find these pressure points is actually quite simple: you just have to ask. People are generally very willing to tell you what is wrong, and it can be a productive and cathartic process. There is often surprisingly little visibility of issues through the strata of management. It takes a formal exercise to cut through the layers and get people to share what frustrates them, slows them down and stops them being as productive as they can be.

The skill is in asking the right people from a sufficiently diverse range of perspectives. Your opinions obviously matter here but your colleagues', partners' and, ideally, customers' opinions matter much more. Get people at every level of seniority in the business. Try to get real diversity in the types of people you speak to. Each time you run the Intersections exercise, consider gathering feedback from a different group of people and maybe use different techniques, for example:

- Run a focus group of colleagues from different areas of the business and different levels of seniority.
- Use email survey tools to collect anonymous feedback from across the business.
- Gather customer feedback data from the marketing department.
- Contact three partners and ask them for their feedback.

Here are some examples of questions you need to ask staff in order to elicit the right feedback:

- What frustrates you most at work?
- What stops you doing your best work each day?
- What are your colleagues' biggest gripes and concerns?
- What are your customers' biggest complaints?
- What do you think keeps the chief executive up at night?

It is often valuable to ask people for their opinion about different scales of the business. Ask them about themselves (*What frustrates you?*), their colleagues (*What is the biggest issue for your team?*), their function, and the company as a whole. Even ask them for their opinion on the industry.

For customers and partners, you should ask them what frustrates them about you and your business. What gets in the way of a great experience, or of doing more business together? Do not trust the opinions of your customer relations or partner managers to get this feedback. Not because they might lie to you, but because I have frequently found that they lie to themselves or fail to hear what the customer or partner is saying. One client sent me to interview its largest and – apparently – happiest customer. The customer told me they were in the process of leaving the supplier and had been trying to tell them for months. This information had never got past the mental filters of the account manager dealing with them.

The most important thing is gathering a diverse range of inputs. You don't have to gather them all in one go. This exercise is meant to last only one day at most. But over time, listen to lots of different people in order to get the most complete overview of your company's pressure points.

External pressure points

External pressure points are those that affect everyone in your industry. They come from factors that are usually beyond your control. For example, raw material costs and availability, regulation, tax, rents, standards, the economy, political uncertainty.

Writing about these pressures in the form of blog posts, white papers and reports, as well as suggesting possible solutions, is a solid route to thought-leadership and the basis of good content-driven marketing campaigns.

Uncovering external pressure points is often a case of doing some solid desk research. Get hold of the key analyst reports covering your sector, the industry magazines and websites, the business pages of the national press. Build up relationships with some of the leading journalists and analysts covering your sector. Talk to your peers through relevant industry bodies. What is on the agenda at your sector's annual conferences? These are the main external pressure points and they are usually well recognized if not always well understood.

Consider:

- What are the biggest issues in the media that cover your sector?
- What's wrong with your supply chain that also affects your peers?
- What downstream issues affect you and your peers?
- What keeps your investors/stakeholders up at night?

Gather all the sources you can lay your hands (or your cursor) on, and every time you find an issue, add it to a tally chart or spreadsheet. Keep a note of how many times various matters arise, and how much coverage is devoted to them. Maybe print or photocopy each article about a topic and keep a file. Whatever method works for you.

Examples of external issues might include:

- regulation/deregulation,
- changing customer behaviour,
- margin pressure based on price competition or materials costs,
- macroeconomic factors,
- skills shortages.

Gather and filter

Between the internal and external pressure points, you will likely identify ten or more relevant issues relatively quickly. Then your challenge is to begin to work out which to focus on first. Pick those that seem the most pressing or have the greatest potential impact. Remember, you don't have to address them all in the first exercise. You will be doing this again in six months' time.

Once you have your filtered list of pressure points, you can move on to the next stage.

Macro trends

Lots of people will tell you (and your clients) that technology-driven change is important. But that, in itself, is not very useful. You need to know the means by which that change is driven.

Through my work across a variety of sectors in the past three years I have identified five 'vectors of change' by which technology transforms companies and markets over and over again. I believe that you can best understand technology-driven change by examining these five macro trends: (high-frequency) change, choice, power, speed and shape.

For each of these trends below I will provide a brief description and overview, then highlight the following:

- **Key effects:** What this trend does to businesses, for example shortening the time a product will remain competitive in the market.
- **Primary business areas affected:** The functions or processes in your business that will be most affected by this trend.
- **Risk factors:** The business traits and behaviours that I know are evidence that a company may be particularly at risk from the effects of this trend.
- **Key takeaways:** The most important things you need to know about each trend in simple, bullet-point form.

I will do my best to distil each trend down to its simplest points. The aim is to help you show how each trend is likely to intersect with the pressure points that you have identified.

High-frequency change

Technology lowers friction in commerce, and particularly innovation, allowing the rapid development and commercialization of new products and services. These new developments frequently come from new entrants to the market rather than established competitors, disrupting the established market pattern and incumbent suppliers. Where previously these new challengers may have been excluded by capital or technical challenges, the lower cost of development, the broad sharing of knowledge, the global workforce and markets enabled by technology now allow them to breach those barriers.

- **Key effects:** Disruptive market change appears on the near horizon, requiring increased time and investment in foresight, strategy and horizon scanning, as well as greater agility in the response.
- **Primary business areas affected:** Planning and strategy processes, budgeting, forecasting, research and development, new product development, growth, continuous process improvement, capital investment.
- **Risk factors:** Lack of formalized and frequent foresight and horizon-scanning activity, long-serving and happy staff with lack of new ideas, too friendly with non-executive directors and board.
- **Key takeaways:** Product lifetimes get shorter | Adoption happens faster | Business models get replaced more quickly | Company lifecycle shortened.

Choice: more competition, more complexity

By lowering the barriers between people and markets, between ideas and reality, technology simply creates more. More competition, more routes to customers, more noise surrounding the signal.

We are approaching a future characterized not by one paradigm or even binary choices but by fractured markets, cultures and power systems. In almost every ecosystem I examine, the range of models, channels, suppliers, partners, audiences and choices is destined to be much greater than before. This presents a new set of challenges – and opportunities – in every market I see.

Your organization is going to be challenged to operate in a more diverse environment, where there are more suppliers, using more models to deliver a greater variety of products. You will be asked to support a more diverse range of customers with very different needs and preferences, via more varied routes to those customers.

- **Key effects:** Competitive challenge drives churn and puts pressure on pricing and margins, for you and your suppliers. Increased market complexity confuses customers and makes new challenges for marketers and buyers.
- **Primary business areas affected:** Sales, marketing, procurement, channel partners and distributors.
- **Risk factors:** Low margin/commodity item businesses; low customer engagement/brand value; overconfidence in monopoly/leadership positions.
- **Key takeaways:** New suppliers | New competitors | New distributors | New communication channels.

Power: everyone is augmented

Technology allows everyone to do more with less. In many cases that may mean we need fewer people. And while whole jobs may not be replaced, much work will be. This trend affects every field of work from professional services to logistics to construction to call centres.

Every person in an organization will have higher reliance on technology, but they will also be more valuable: if there are fewer people for the same turnover, then every person is inherently worth more to the business. This will maintain the battle for top talent and increase the value we place on the most powerful human skills, particularly discovery, creativity and communication.

- **Key effects:** Augmentation, automation.
- **Primary business areas affected:** Workforce, capital investments in technology and plant.
- **Risk factors:** Overstaffing, lack of tech investment and knowledge.
- **Key takeaways:** Automation | Augmentation | Fewer people, each of higher value.

Speed: we want everything right now

In the mid-noughties the stats suggested that if your website didn't load in seven seconds, you would lose half of your visitors. Today sites are expected to load in a few hundred milliseconds. As technology has stripped the friction from many of our day-to-day interactions, so we expect all others to be equally fast. From same-day delivery to live chatbots answering every inquiry in seconds.

This trend translates into business behaviour. We expect our supplier, partners or investments to be on the ball, able to pull in information from us or the market, process it and return a decision, or better a solution, in a matter of moments.

- **Key effects:** Customer, market, investor expectations.
- **Primary business areas affected:** Customer services, decision-making, partner relations, investor relations, regulator relations.
- **Risk factors:** Centralized and slow decision-making, aggregated bureaucracy, CYA (cover your ass) culture.
- **Key takeaway:** Technology raises expectations for the speed of response, from customers, partners, investors and regulators.

Shape: networks not monoliths

When the friction between business functions is lower, there is less need to house them all under the same roof, either physically or legally. This is true of our workers as well. The result is that more and more organizations are dissolving their previously monolithic structures in favour of more fluid arrangements, involving networks of partners and freelancers or distributed shared functions inside the business. The prime example, pardon the pun, is Amazon, a company composed entirely of distributed functional blocks that can be leveraged by business lines both inside and outside the company. Consider Amazon Web Services, formerly an internal IT function and now one of the largest cloud hosting companies in the world and responsible for the bulk of Amazon's profits. Amazon scales its logistics engine by engaging self-employed workers and taking the friction out of them running their own business.

- **Key effects:** Technology breaks down barriers and streamlines interfaces, changing the natural shape of organizations.
- **Primary business areas affected:** HR, organization design, financial structure, procurement policies.
- **Risk factors:** Conservative culture, monolithic organizational design, risk aversion.
- **Key takeaways:** Networks not monoliths | Loosely coupled components.

Finding your intersections

The next stage in the process is to look for intersections between the five macro trends above and the pressure points you identified earlier.

Take one of your pressure points and think about the effects each trend might have upon it. Consider for each pressure point the following questions:

- Will this INCREASE the pressure?
- Will this DECREASE the pressure?
- Will this CREATE a new opportunity?

The answer is often 'yes' to more than one of these for each pressure point, particularly for market-wide pressures where the company that rapidly finds a solution may have a clear advantage.

Take the example of a client who realized they had a major issue with internal communications and the flow of information through the business. As one member of staff put it during the interviews I conducted: 'We have a chasing culture here.

Nothing happens unless I pick up the phone.' This was despite the company having invested in technology to automate the flow of order and stock information through the business. Because the company had not invested in culture change alongside the new technology, people were bypassing the systems and relying on the phone – or often waiting for the call – before acting. This was slowing down the rate at which the business processed orders, costing significant administrative time and making it less responsive to customer demands.

How does this pressure point map this against the five macro trends?

- **High-frequency change:** Information moving slowly through the organization will absolutely affect the company's ability to respond to market trends, though this was more of an issue with operational information than strategic decision-making.
- **Increased choice:** No major intersection here, other than that the company will be facing more competitors who will likely be more effective at moving information around and so be more responsive to customers.
- **Augmented power:** A big intersection here. As everyone in the company's industry adopts more technology to automate processes and augment their people, a company that lacks a culture of technology adoption and still relies too heavily on person-to-person interactions is going to be rapidly left behind.
- **Accelerated speed:** A huge intersection again here. The biggest impact of this pressure point was slow customer responses, in a world where expectations are rising ever faster. Unaddressed, this would be a huge competitive disadvantage and a likely platform for competitors and

new entrants to challenge their dominant market position.

- **Networked shape:** Some strategic impact here. If the company was reliant on calls to communicate internally, then it was likely to have the same issue in its interactions with customers, partners and the rest of its supply chain (something that came out in a separate pressure point identified through interviews with customers).

The primary intersection between macro trends and pressure points, then, was that in the near future what was already an issue with slow internal communication was likely to become critical, perhaps even an existential threat, as customer expectations for speed of communication rose, and the level of automation and augmentation across the industry increased. The pressure at an existing point was likely to increase significantly, driven by the macro trends.

The reverse does happen: sometimes the macro trends alleviate an existing pressure. For example, one client had major issues with its margins because of the level of manual information processing it had to handle. But the power trend made it absolutely clear that a lot of that processing could soon be automated at very low cost. They could then plot a path towards appropriate investment in technology and redirect the staff they had doing manual processing into sales roles.

Likewise, sometimes the process will throw up entirely new opportunities, particularly where the pressure point is something felt by all the existing competitors in a particular industry. If you can see how a macro trend will alleviate – or exacerbate – that issue, and be the first to respond, you can carve out a lead.

Having mapped your pressure points against the macro trends, you should find yourself with a list of intersections. The next challenge is filtering these intersections and identifying those that present the greatest threat or opportunity. Sometimes the number of intersections that result from the mapping process is quite large. You cannot address them all and you should not try. Over time I have come up with two different approaches to filtering your intersections: scaling and sorting. Use these to filter your intersections so that you can focus on the most important.

Do not be afraid to discount some issues at this stage. If they are truly significant, they will reoccur when you run this exercise again. If at the end of the scaling-and-sorting process you are still concerned about the number of apparently significant issues to be addressed, consider running the exercise again in three months rather than six.

But first, see if these approaches help you to focus.

Scaling: marginal and exponential

One means of sorting your intersections is to try to put a rough scale on their impact. This doesn't work for all intersections – for example, it is often hard to scale those that intersect with the shape trend. But for issues to do with choice, speed and power, it can be a valuable approach.

To begin scaling your intersections, choose a metric that would be a measure of its impact. For example, will this intersection affect profit, margins or revenue? Each of these can be measured in numerical terms. Will it affect the number of people you need to recruit each year? Or perhaps the lifecycle for each iteration of your product and hence the frequency with which you need to retool? All of these can have numerical estimates put upon them.

These numbers don't have to be precise, just to within an order of magnitude – i.e. is it units, tens, hundreds, thousands or tens of thousands? Or, put another way, is it one in five, one in fifty or one in five hundred? The reason for this scaling will soon become clear.

Once you have selected a metric, see if you can determine how great the impact of the intersection might be upon it. Again, we are not trying to be precise. We just need to get within one order of magnitude. So, will the effect be 1, 10, 100 or 1,000 per cent?

For example:

- Imagine you are looking at the effect of the power trend on an existing workforce challenge. You can put a number on the workforce, or perhaps those employed in a specific discipline (e.g. call-centre operators). Will automation cut the size of this workforce by 0.5 per cent, 5 per cent or 50 per cent?
- With the choice trend, new competition might put pressure on your margins. Again, you can put a number on your profit margin. Might a new market entrant undercutting you reduce your margins by 1 per cent, 10 per cent or 100 per cent?

What you are looking for are intersections that have a scale of impact factor above 50 per cent. Unless it is going to at least halve or double your profit margin, workforce or any other metric, you can treat it as marginal. For example, if you believe a change will be +/–20 per cent, mark it as marginal. This may seem like a big change, but you should find that many of your intersections have possible impacts in the higher ranges.

Sometimes you might put extreme ranges on these numbers. Don't be afraid to do so. Consider the cost difference that the internet made to music retail. Digital music retailers required no shipping, no high-street stores and, by my estimates, 200 times fewer staff. If you had been running an Intersections exercise for music retailers in the mid-noughties, you would have been putting some pretty extreme numbers on the impact on profit margin, workforce and more.

Sorting: urgent, important, existential

Created by President Eisenhower and popularized by Stephen Covey in *The 7 Habits of Highly Successful People*, the Urgent/ Important matrix is a useful method of organizing your to-do list and separating out the tasks of true leadership from the day-to-day commitments that can often overwhelm you and prevent you from thinking strategically. We can also use this method to sort our intersections. This approach is useful for those intersections that feel important but that are hard to put a clear scale on.

Again we use a 2 x 2 matrix, with 'Urgent' and 'Not urgent' on one axis and 'Operational' and 'Existential' on the other.

- Operational issues have a marginal impact on business as usual. They might be challenging and disruptive, but they don't present a serious threat to the business, or an opportunity to create a new one. These issues can be funnelled into existing procedures and dealt with accordingly.
- Existential issues might lead to the end of the existing business, or permit the creation of a new one. These are the issues that need a new type of response, and if they are urgent, a rapid one.

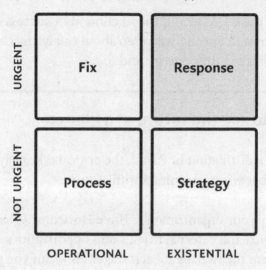

See if you can place your intersections on this plan. You are only interested in the issues that make it into the existential boxes. Anything else can be filtered out and passed into existing systems for project development or issue resolution.

Final five

Whether you chose the scaling or sorting route, the aim is to end up with roughly five intersections on which you are going to take action in this round. If you have many more than five, you should go back to the process or leave some for a second wave of actions. Even the largest and most resource-rich organizations will struggle to address more than a few truly exponential opportunities or existential threats at one time. Tempting as it is to address them all, it is worth filtering again at this stage to focus on the five (or fewer) with the greatest impact.

Trying to address too many issues at once can diminish the

impact of the exercise and the likelihood of success of any actions that result. Foresight is often about catalysing change, and this catalysis requires energy and focus.

How to see the future at a glance

Here is a distillation of Part 2, the critical takeaways to remember when planning for the future:

- Study your organization's 'Three Horizons'. What internal and external threats and opportunities will present themselves at each stage? How can you prepare for them?
- Use scenario planning every few years to determine your long-term strategy and direction.
- Build the Intersections model into your day-to-day functioning. Examine the incoming opportunities and threats to your organization or sector every six months.

Part 3 Rapid Response

Now that you have some tactics for gathering and deciphering the clues in the data to safeguard your future, the next section will help you ready your organization to act rapidly on what you've learned.

3.1 Making the Right Decisions, Faster

How long does it take your organization to make decisions? In a business world of high-frequency change, most people feel that their answer is 'too long'. From the simplest leave approval or sign-off of expenses, to strategic decisions about entering a new market or investing in a new product, I hear complaints from people across client organizations that things just happen too slowly. And if it is not the client complaining, it is often the customer.

Slow decision-making presents two distinct threats. There is a clear competitive threat: if you are too slow to make critical strategic leaps to address risks or opportunities, then you can be outpaced by competitors – particularly the nimbler new entrants who have wrong-footed many major names in recent years, whether that is in media (Netflix), banking (Starling) or automotive (Tesla). And there is the risk to your customer relationship. As some research I undertook with Demandware (now Salesforce Commerce Cloud) in 2016 showed, speed of service is one of the highest priorities for retail customers, and I strongly believe this priority is shared with customers in a business-to-business environment. We want everything right now!

I will show how you can future-proof your business by accelerating decision-making in two ways. Firstly, by pushing power to the edge of the organization and empowering people at the edge to make you more responsive. Secondly, by improving the supply of good information to leaders like you to support more rapid strategic decisions.

Two-speed thinking

Building a culture of rapid response is vital to surviving in the long term and the key to this is good decision-making at all levels. But the best decisions are not always the fastest. Sometimes, slower, data-based, strategic decisions are required. Knowing when to tell the difference is key. Like the two speeds of human thinking identified by Amos Tversky and Daniel Kahneman,[1] businesses must have two distinct decision-making speeds:

Speed 1 – Operational Decision-Making. This is the day-to-day activity of business; decisions on customer credit, sales, negotiations, leave approvals and even hiring decisions. Here, any delay is detrimental to customer service and business performance. Decisions made on these kinds of tasks should be fast, intuitive and automatic.

Speed 2 – Strategic Decision-Making. We apply this style of thinking when considering more expansive, strategy-based questions like whether to invest in a new direction for the business or to expand into a new market or the selection of a key partner. It is slow, deliberate and difficult. It requires the contemplation of diverse and sometimes conflicting opinions and data. Here, the challenge is not to make the decision quickly but to make the best decision with all the data available. For both methods of decision-making thinking, those engaged should be conscious of which speed they are working to before engaging with the task at hand.

Whether your team is thinking in speed 1 or 2, the challenge in many cases is to get the information to the decision-maker as early as possible. But we can start by understanding how fast that information flows today, first for operational decisions.

Accessing agility – operational decision-making

What slows down decisions in your organization today? I hear many stories of sclerotic bureaucracy or people deferring decisions because they just do not feel they have the confidence or authority to take them. Does your organization suffer from these issues?

Using the questions about internal pressure points listed earlier in the book, carry out a survey of members of staff in your organization on the pressure points they face when performing their operational duties. Some clear signs of unnecessary red tape might be:

- 'It takes too long to get customer credit approved. The request has to be passed to my boss, and then my boss's boss.'
- 'Just getting sign-off for a half-day's leave needs three signatures and I have to spend ages chasing managers. Why can't my boss just say yes or no?'

- 'Turning around a decision on merchandising can take three days by the time all the appropriate people have signed off the decision. It means we can't respond fast enough to news and events.'
- 'We have committees upon committees. Every piece of information has to flow through at least three people before it reaches someone who will take a decision, and by then both the urgency and the meaning have often been destroyed.'

These are all real-world examples based on the feedback I have received when working inside client organizations, or from people who have attended my training courses. They come from all sorts of companies: a law firm, a small furniture manufacturer, a supermarket and a software company. Typically, the older a company is, the more layers of bureaucracy have built up and the less time people spend questioning the reason for those layers. They are just the way things are, until someone points out that things do not have to be that way.

Take this example that was relayed to me during a workshop with a global manufacturer by a member of its finance team:

A few years ago, our business was struggling with the administrative load around the sales process. Due to an issue with a bad debt many years previously, we had set a low credit limit for new sales. For any deal larger than this, the salesperson had to get sign-off from multiple, more senior managers. This was slowing the response to customers and consuming too much sales and admin resource.

I was tasked with tackling this problem. At first, I looked at software systems that might streamline the flow of information. But I soon realized the simplest solution was to raise the credit limit. It didn't have to be raised much to dramatically cut the number of deals that needed enhanced approval, immediately speeding our customer response times and freeing time for the salespeople, executives and administrators who were processing the workload.

Your colleagues across your organization may have stories like this that a simple pressure-points examination might reveal. Identifying these problems is the first step towards addressing your operational decision-making obstacles and dealing with them. If you want to dig into this issue further, here are some good places to look for problems:

- **Expenses processing:** How much time is lost between executives and the finance team in processing expenses? This is time that could valuably be used elsewhere and a source of disgruntlement for employees.
- **Order handling:** How much data re-entry is involved in the order-to-shipping/order-to-pay processes? I have frequently found that leaders believe a problem solved because they have invested in software and hardware, but the reality on the ground is a mishmash of workarounds.
- **Budget approval:** One of the biggest time-sinks in the finance department is often assembling the annual budget. This remains, in many organizations, a nightmare of spreadsheet wrangling and interdepartmental rancour.
- **New employee onboarding:** New employees are frequently subjected to the worst excesses of corporate bureaucracy as they bounce through multiple

conversations and forms to get themselves
online, working and acclimatized to all the new
systems.

These are just a few examples. They are stones to turn over
to see what you find. It is far from a complete list of where the
issues lie, but it is a good bet that if you find problems here, you
will find them elsewhere in the organization as well.

You can try to rectify individually each of the issues that are
revealed in the pressure-points exercise, but if there are many,
it may suggest a broader, cultural problem in the business. One
of the key causes is the over-centralization of power, which will
be covered in section 3.2.

Strategic decision-making speed

How about your strategic decision-making? How fast, and how
confidently, do you make big decisions? How much time is
spent on the decision itself and how much on gathering the
evidence and arguments to support it? How much are those
decisions based on hard data and how much on intuition and
gut feeling? The ideal situation is for decisions to be based on
both empirical evidence and human judgement. Hard data will
rarely give you the entire picture. A willingness to make calls
based on experience and instincts is unlikely to stop being part
of a leader's make-up any time soon. But we do work in a world
where better data are increasingly available. Those data can also
be more easily presented in a comprehensible and compelling
form. Instinct may be the ultimate decider, but there is no ar-
gument for making decisions without the data if they are
available.

Think about these scenarios:

- Your company is considering entering a new country.
- Your company is considering investing in a new product line.
- Your company is considering raising investment.

For each of those scenarios consider these questions:

- How rich are the data that support your decision-making?
- How long did the relevant information take to collate and present?
- How confident are you in the quality and transparency of the data?

In each scenario, a proportion of the data required to drive the decision will come from inside the organization, from your finance systems, marketing data and operational systems, such as stock control. A proportion will come from outside, whether that is market research, analyst reports, partners and suppliers or external consultants. These data will usually be passed through multiple hands before they reach the ultimate decision-maker, resulting in two problems common in far too many of the organizations I have encountered.

First, the collation and presentation of the data takes a long time. It is an enormous manual effort, usually laid on members of the finance or marketing teams. The data are in the company systems but often held in disparate places and in a variety of formats. There are also varying levels of confidence in the data. According to a survey of global chief financial officers by the software company Prophix,[2] just 20 per cent have complete confidence in the data in their systems, while 60 per cent say they 'mostly' trust the data in their systems, meaning that every time they are called upon to answer a business question, much fact-checking and verification is required. This is perhaps not surprising, given that the same study showed that a quarter of companies still keep all their financial data in a disparate collection of spreadsheets!

Second, the data are often shaped into a narrative that supports the beliefs or interests of the people looking to drive the decision. Sometimes this is for the avoidance of negative outcomes for the person preparing or approving the data (once described to me as CYA, or cover your ass, interventions). If the data show underperformance of a unit, its head might look to insert mitigating factors or even soften the numbers by tweaking the period they cover or including additional revenue streams. This may sound rather fraudulent on the face of it, but the person concerned may be absolutely convinced that this is how they present a fair picture of the situation. Sometimes the data are 'shaped' to present a clearer case for a particular plan. Again, this may not be deliberate fraud but rather the person presenting the most compelling story for a plan in which they wholeheartedly believe.

The result of these two factors combined is that the decisions themselves are often delayed and predicated on less-than-transparent evidence. How do you know if this is the case in your organization? Here are some clues:

- If you ask for a report on a particular slice of
  performance data and are told that they will have
  to schedule some analyst time to produce it,
  then the people doing the analysis are likely
  overworked or underequipped. Probably both.

(The ideal scenario is that you can self-serve with this information.)

- If the reports that you receive are excessively polished in terms of their presentation, this can also be a bad sign. What you want is clear and unambiguous charts or numbers with perhaps a little narrative around them. If instead you are getting a sixteen-slide PowerPoint presentation, there is quite possibly too much thought going into the story that the numbers are telling.

Sometimes the interference in your data happens before they even reach your business. Such as in the case when the managing director of a PR agency asked me to take a look at his business and offer some pointers on future-proofing. This was a successful, profitable agency with a great track record on delivering results for clients. But there is always room for improvement.

I started with a pressure-points analysis, interviewing all the staff via an email survey. What immediately became clear was that staff were spending an inordinate amount of time communicating with clients, and particularly on providing reports. Much of this reporting was the re-presentation of reports that they had in turn received from an external media-monitoring agency.

Communicating with the client is clearly important, but in many cases, people were spending twice as much time communicating results as actually achieving them. This had a negative impact both on the agency's performance in terms of results delivered and on its potential profit margins, as well as on the return on investment for the client.

I recommended that the agency stopped re-presenting results and directed all coverage directly to the client, highlighting the transparency this demonstrated, as well as automating some other reporting tasks.

Consider your organization. In the scenarios above, would you get the right information to decide, fast and untainted? Or would the decision be delayed and unduly influenced by slow, poor-quality or overly shaped evidence? How far would the information need to travel from source to the decision-maker? Could that have an effect on the transparency of that data?

Better operations drive better strategy

One thing you may have noticed from many of the examples of poor operational decision-making is that the problem flows uphill. When junior people at the edges of organizations are not given enough autonomy and responsibility they turn to their seniors. This eats away at management time, leaving less room to focus on the critical existential challenges for the business and wider strategic thinking.

Underinvestment in the processes and technologies that underpin operational activities has a similarly corrosive effect on strategic decision-making. If the finance team is completely consumed closing the annual accounts, producing reports or wrestling with the budget, they have much less time for forecasting, financial scenario planning or advising the rest of the business on trends they have extracted from the numbers. Prophix's survey of chief financial officers showed that in 10 per cent of organizations the budgeting cycle ties up the finance team for more than three months. A further 43 per cent of organizations acknowledged that the process took too long. The same problems abound elsewhere in the business. If the warehouse still runs on an analogue process that involves passing bits of paper around, there will be a lack of transparency through the system. There will be a lag in critical information. It is impossible to disconnect operational from strategic decision-making for these reasons.

Assessing decision-making

Ultimately, there are five questions to ask yourself about the speed of decision-making in your business:

How far does information have to travel through your organization before it reaches a decision-maker? Pick a single information flow, whether that is operational (for example, credit approval) or strategic (investment approval in product development) and count the number of steps, or the hands, that the proposal is passed through.

How fast does that journey happen? This can be measured in hours (or, more likely, days or even weeks).

How much are the data interfered with as they make their journey? How many opportunities are there for the information to be reinterpreted or re-presented? For example, is the same report passed up through the chain (in which case the opportunities for interference are limited) or are the data extracted and re-presented in PowerPoint presentations or more glossy reports with more narrative?

How much work is required to extract meaning from the data? Is your corporate data – e.g. sales numbers, marketing analytics, financial reports – readily accessible and easy to manipulate in order to answer business questions?

Is the ultimate decision taken in a timely fashion? Once the evidence is presented, how fast is the decision made, and are there unnecessary delays and procrastinations due to lack of corporate confidence or clear lines of responsibility?

Ask these questions of your organization and you are likely to identify some of the key issues that limit the speed and acuity of decision-making in the business.

3.2 Empowering People to Perform

> You can't run a large business with a command-and-control approach these days. It is simply too slow and inefficient. The only way to respond to what customers want and what the market demands is to empower your people with responsibility and autonomy.
>
> As a leader you must take responsibility for the change of culture this requires. That means ensuring your people have the skills, the guidance and the tools to take decisions. And then, crucially, backing them up when they make those calls – whether they are right or wrong. If they took a decision within the bounds that you laid down, you have to demonstrate to the rest of the business that they did the right thing. Otherwise all you will do is perpetuate a culture of fear where no one takes responsibility.
>
> Ian Stuart, CEO, HSBC UK

Now that you've assessed how agile your decision-making is in your organization, you can start to look at ways to streamline these processes. The simplest way to approach this is by devolving power from a top-down command-and-control hierarchy to decision-makers located as close to the market and customer as possible. This may be the cheapest and most effective way to improve the speed of response to market signals and customer requests. This is not to say that devolving power is a cost-free exercise. It has implications for your recruitment and your training. And it certainly carries risks, making it a challenging prospect.

Many leaders are used to operating in a culture where power is centralized. Where responsibility can be handed up the chain and where the simple expedient of having several pairs of eyes on a question before it is answered is used to mitigate the risk of the final answer being wrong. A culture of devolved decision-making looks very different from what we are familiar and comfortable with. Even if we decide it is the right approach, and to pursue it, we first must engender an entrepreneurial culture in which leadership and innovation from the bottom up is prized in order to motivate staff to take up responsibility.

Some companies are already there, the German supermarket chains Aldi and Lidl being prime examples. People attribute their unprecedented growth over the last few years (Aldi grew store numbers in the UK nearly 50 per cent between 2013 and 2017[3]) to low prices and an absence of frills. But people tend to miss just how important these companies' culture of delegation has been to their success. In an interview, Aldi Scotland's MD Richard Holloway said:

Aldi's area management graduate scheme is not for those who lack confidence. Just 14 weeks into the year-long training programme, you could be managing your own store. Following the programme, you typically manage three to four stores. Those graduates who are natural leaders and thrive on challenge are probably best suited to the scheme, as it has an unusually high level of responsibility for graduate retail management schemes and a training programme that its own graduates have called 'demanding'.[4]

Aldi and Lidl succeed by distributing power to the edges of their organizations – power on which their employees 'thrive', even if it is an extremely challenging environment. The overwhelming weight of stories that I am told and cultures that I experience are predicated on a few powerful people steering the operations of many more. But this may be changing, in part because it must.

Collaborative leadership

The devolution of power to the edges of the business has a natural corollary. Not only do we empower people to utilize their ability to act in relation to our customers and partners, we give them the confidence to feed back into the business. Over the last few years this change has formed part of a growing culture of collaborative leadership.

We used to see business leaders as strong and decisive, pursuing their own vision and driving the company forward through sheer force of will. But this is a risky approach in an age of complexity and ambiguity. Our markets and our companies are more diverse now. There is more information at hand than ever before. And there are more opportunities and risks. No individual can process them all. So, smart leaders are accepting that the best approach is not always to command but often to question. To draw on the expertise across the business and let other people filter the enormous range of signals and possibilities for them.

Wherever you are in the leadership hierarchy you can start to implement some of the lessons of collaborative leadership. There are three simple steps:

1 **Get comfortable with the phrase 'I don't know'.** You don't have to say it out loud to others if it makes you uncomfortable. At least, not at first. But recognize that it is OK not to have the answers as a leader and to draw those answers from your team.

2 **Ask more questions.** Show your team that you value not only their work but their expertise, opinions and unique perspective.

3 **Listen to, and act on, the answers.** Demonstrate that people's contributions are valuable by showing you have listened, considering their input and feeding back. Share the reasons for your ultimate course of action and give credit where it is due for steering you.

Sharing autonomy and responsibility

What we want from work is an opportunity to succeed, to demonstrate our value, and to be rewarded for it, both financially and with personal approbation. We feel good when we do good work, and that work should attract good feedback. Doing good work and delivering value to our maximum potential requires two things: responsibility and autonomy.

Responsibility means the ownership of problems. Autonomy means the freedom to determine the solution to those problems. If we have responsibility without autonomy, we are always following someone else's instructions. While we might be worked hard, we can never extend ourselves and grow. If we

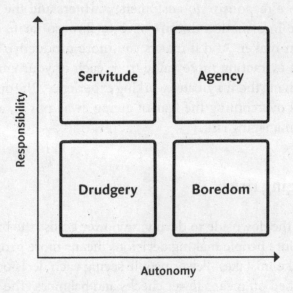

have autonomy without responsibility, it is a recipe for boredom. We have the freedom to do nothing, and no opportunity to deliver value. Without responsibility or autonomy, we might as well be small children. But with both, we have the opportunity to pursue a fulfilling and rewarding career.

Future-proof businesses aim to give all their employees both responsibility and autonomy because doing so maximizes the value of employment for the employee. We all want happy, motivated employees.

A study from the University of Birmingham showed that employees with higher levels of autonomy in their work reported positive effects on their overall well-being and higher levels of job satisfaction.[5] Unfortunately, the research also highlighted that, despite the benefits, managers remain unwilling to offer employees greater levels of autonomy because their primary role remains one of 'control and effort extraction'.

Pushing power out to the edge of your organization makes

you more responsive to customers, partners and the market, because information doesn't have to flow so far to reach a decision-maker. And it makes you more productive because you are extracting more value from each of your employees while giving them a greater working experience. The only challenge is overcoming the fear of giving away power, and that means managing risk.

Managing risk

What's the downside to devolving power across the business? Risk. More people making decisions means more people who can make mistakes. Fewer people seeing each decision before it is signed off means fewer checks and balances. The benefits of distributing power are enormous, but only if these risks can be offset. Managing this risk is the critical investment in delegation. Doing so has six aspects: rules, trust and support (when delegating responsibility), confidence, authority and skills (when delegating autonomy).

Rules

A crucial first step when devolving power away from the centre is to define where responsibility lies in the new system. Each newly empowered member of staff will need to know exactly what their responsibilities are and what boundaries they have to operate within. This will need to be documented and communicated clearly to everyone involved; to each member of staff, their line managers and the senior leadership team.

When making decisions that are at the edge of their boundaries, people need clear lines of communication to their managers. If the delegation has been effective, then the managers should have a reduced workload and more time to address those queries.

What might these boundaries be? Here are some examples:

- Budget expenditure – single item or total expenditure in period.
- Sales discounts.
- Customer credit decisions.
- Partner appointments.
- Marketing messages – e.g. creating content for social media.
- Complaint resolution.

These may look obvious, but many businesses still subject these processes to surprising levels of centralization, as I showed in the examples in section 3.1.

Trust

If you are going to be releasing power to people across the business, you need to trust them. Partly this is your own issue: releasing control is hard and you will be unlikely to have a one-to-one relationship with everyone who is being empowered to take decisions. This is why the processes and structures that you put in place are so important. You may not be able to put your trust in every individual personally, but you should be able to put your trust in the systems and processes that surround them.

The bigger issues might be the trust of middle managers in their junior reports. As the previously referenced study from the University of Birmingham showed, managers frequently see their role as one of 'control and effort extraction' as opposed to offering empowerment and support. Perhaps it is here where the greatest training and development need sits.

Support

What happens when someone makes a bad decision? When they use the autonomy they have been given and something goes wrong? The answer must be that they are supported. That they are given the clear and unambiguous backing of both their line manager and the senior leadership. As long as they were operating inside the boundaries that had been set, they must be praised for making a decision. Because to do anything else would be to kill any nascent culture of entrepreneurialism and shared responsibility. It would instil fear in people about taking decisions.

That is not to say that the person who made the error should not have to rectify it. Or that perhaps changes may be needed to rules, policies or training. But in many cases very little change may be required. Things go wrong in business. We learn from them. Everyone in the company should learn from what went wrong. But the cost of this error must be measured against the alternative: slow, sclerotic, unchanging business that creates costs for both the company and the customer.

People given responsibility and autonomy need to know that they can make mistakes without any single error being a career-limiting issue. But they also need lines of support to minimize the chances of those mistakes happening in the first place: clear lines of communication with senior leaders, constantly updated guidance and training, and peer-to-peer support as well – something that can be an enormous source of learning and confidence.

Confidence

Are your people confident in their ability to operate autonomously? This is clearly an individual issue and each person will need different amounts of coaching and development to grow their confidence. Anyone who is too confident on day one is as likely to be a risk as an asset. Look at coaching programmes to accelerate development.

Authority

The issue of trust is tied directly to the issue of authority. If people are to exercise power, particularly if they are relatively junior and inexperienced, then the scope of that power has to be understood by those with whom they are interacting. If peers are constantly second-guessing them, or customers are frequently asking to speak to a manager, then there is an issue with someone's authority.

Developing people's confidence is part of the solution. But in some workplaces there still exist cultural issues that cause people to underestimate or even refuse to accept someone's authority because of their age, sex or race. Occasionally such problems will be acute and require sanctions. But there are positive steps you can take early on to change the culture of the business. Ann Francke's book in the Penguin Business Experts series on creating a gender-balanced workplace has tips that could be useful in this context.[6]

Other signifiers of authority can also be helpful. While being fussy about job titles might seem a little petty in this age of networked business and flat hierarchies, they are still an important signifier to many. While that remains the case, they can be a handy way to communicate authority.

Skills

Your staff need to be trained to make use of the responsibility you assign them, and to exercise their autonomy. This may be a set of hard technical skills or soft skills, depending on the changes within their role.

Skills development programmes in my view need to focus on three clear areas:

- **Curation:** Your staff must be adept in the discovery and qualification of information. This covers everything from effective web searching to interrogating customer complaints to understand their root cause, or manipulating data sets to extract meaning and value.
- **Creation:** Your staff need the skills of innovation to build new solutions. They need to know how to test and iterate, to gather feedback and to take existing ideas and recombine them into something new. Contrary to popular belief, the skills of creativity can be taught.
- **Communication:** Your staff need to be able to sell their ideas and solutions, both to the customer and to their line managers. That means having the confidence and competence to communicate effectively, whether that is in written, spoken or even visual form.

Few corporate training and development programmes in my experience focus on these highly transferable soft skills. Yet they are increasingly critical to the work of almost everyone in business.

Checklist: responsibility and autonomy

Here is a summary of the six things that must be present if people within your organization are to take responsibility and operate semi-autonomously, and what to do if they are not:

Responsibility	Autonomy

Rules

Are the limits of their responsibility clear? Do they understand the consequences of straying beyond those limits?

Action: *If the answer is no, then either rules need (re)writing or they need to be better communicated. However, rules also need to be reviewed as people grow in their role so that they can continue to stretch.*

Confidence

Are they confident in their own ability to operate autonomously?

Action: *Additional training or support may be required, perhaps shadowing a more senior colleague or paired working for a period.*

Trust

Do they have your confidence and that of their line managers, peers and reports?

Action: *Responsibility must be given as well as taken. If line managers are micro-managing, it is very hard for someone to step up and take responsibility. Ensure reviews allow for the capture of such issues and incorporate appropriate instruction into management training.*

Authority

Is their power to act clear to colleagues, partners and customers?

Action: *There are multiple indicators of authority, not all of them deliberate or positive. For example, some people will still be dismissive of people based on age, sex or race. If this is the case with other staff, then it needs to be countered with appropriate sanctions. Where it is harder to address directly, for example with customers, look at ways to help staff show they have authority in their domain with signifiers such as appropriate job titles and skills training around effective communication.*

Responsibility	Autonomy
Support	**Skills**
Even the most autonomous and confident staff need an open line of communication to their superiors to check and confirm some decisions. Ensure these pathways are open and that the message that comes back is always one of support, as long as people are operating inside their boundaries.	No one can act autonomously without the appropriate skills. Training is a core part of extending autonomy to the edge of the organization and it must be ongoing to allow people to continue to grow their capabilities.
Action: Look at communications channels. How available are you or line managers? What is the response time for queries? How is that response communicated? Is it positive?	**Action:** Look at your training programmes. Are they a box-ticking exercise or do they empower people with the skills to act? Not just technical skills but soft skills as well: curation and discovery, creativity and communication.

Devolving power

Releasing power to the edge of the organization and giving people the responsibility and autonomy to exercise it has multiple benefits. Firstly, it shortens the distance that information, inquiries or proposals have to travel before they are dealt with, accelerating your response to operational issues. Secondly, it frees time for more senior managers and leaders, giving them greater scope to focus on more strategic decision-making. And thirdly, it unlocks more resources from your organization and gives your people greater engagement and motivation. The risks it presents have to be managed but they are more than justified by the rewards.

3.3 Hyper-decisive

Leaders must be in a position to steer the organization. Even with more power distributed, someone needs to have oversight of the collective direction of the business. To do that, leaders need access to good information and must have the ability to communicate decisions out to the organization effectively.

PwC's 22nd Annual Global CEO Survey shows the enormity of the gap between the information leaders believe they need in order to make good decisions, and that information's availability.[7] Although 94 per cent say information about customer preferences and needs is critical, just 15 per cent feel they have comprehensive information on that topic; 92 per cent say financial forecasts and projections are critical, but just 41 per cent say they have them. Clearly, the right information is not reaching the right people, either at the right time or in the right form.

Recognizing this, Howard Dresner, former Gartner analyst, founder of Dresner Advisory Services and the man who coined the term 'business intelligence', proposed that companies should aim to become 'hyper-decisive'. He says they must leverage 'information democracy' across the organization to allow decisions to be taken rapidly, by people at all levels, based on solid data. In Dresner's words: 'What we call "hyper-decisiveness" is the ability for an enterprise to instantaneously process vast arrays of data and information and deliver actionable insights to a growing community of users.'[8]

For me, the ideal is that *everyone* with decision-making capability in an organization should be data-literate. Leaders should not be reliant on small numbers of highly skilled people in finance, marketing or strategy functions to do the data analysis for them. That means they need access to the training, and the tools, to extract their own meaning from raw data. And they need the skills to present that data in a coherent, comprehensible and compelling form in order to share its meaning. This has implications for your technology investments, for skills training and for human resources. Who do you hire? How do you train them? And what is the appropriate technology for them to use?

The age of automation and augmentation

Dresner highlights that the processing of data must be 'instantaneous'. You cannot achieve this if the collation of data and the process of translating it into information is the work of months of spreadsheet wrangling. Workers in future-proof organizations need to have good information at their fingertips so that they can steer their businesses effectively. It needs to be available on demand, in real time, not days, weeks or months later.

The only solution to this challenge is to ensure that much of the processing of the data is automatic, not manual. This, again, is why data cannot be the preserve of a few specialists. If you are to extract the maximum value out of data, you need the help of machines.

This highlights an interesting context for this shift: automation and human augmentation.

Extracting answers to business questions from stacks of data across multiple systems is today the job of a specialist. But what if those data are aggregated into one coherent set and then a machine is employed to help extract the meaning that is sought? Then, anyone in the business can find the answers they need with limited skills training.

It has been technically possible for decades to integrate all our various corporate data sources – financial, supply chain, marketing, HR, procurement, etc. – into a single, coherent whole. But it has been both expensive and complex. The result is that large organizations still tend to exist on a mishmash of systems held together by the goodwill and efforts of people with the knowledge and skills to pull them all together at the appropriate moments – for example, in the production of annual budgets or when asked questions by investors or regulators.

But the price of coherence, and the ease of integration, has become more attractive year on year as technologies have matured. Most young enterprises will operate on a single system, developed in house or acquired. Or, more likely, they will use a suite of different systems that were all built with interconnection in mind. Sharing data between them is a natural part of their design, not a bolt-on upgrade. Older enterprises have slowly begun to wrangle all their various data sets into something approaching a coherent whole.

On top of this coherent store of data you can apply the modern tools of data interrogation, be they reporting tools based on a graphical user interface (GUI), corporate performance management systems (CPM) or the latest iterations of business intelligence (BI). Suddenly, you don't have to be a spreadsheet wizard to find the answers you are seeking.

The advent of machine learning takes this process a step further. Now the machine can actively assist you in finding the answers you want. It may even suggest certain analyses based on what it understands about your business.

The human factor

The technologies described above are not futuristic: they are here today. It just takes a long time for us to adopt such technologies to their full potential. After all, most companies are still working out how to extract value from the Office suite that has been around for thirty years! But these technologies cannot offer a complete answer. Technology allows us to collect data in real time, automate some of the processing and present information in a dynamic fashion. But none of this is of value unless our community of users, across the organization, is equipped with the skills to utilize that data to improve the business every day and drive better decisions.

Turning numbers into insight is about the technical challenge of data manipulation and analysis, but it is also about skills of storytelling and narrative. Information democracy can only become real if the skills of data literacy are widespread across the business.

All of us need the skills of discovery and qualification, the ability to recognize gaps in our knowledge and understanding, to source data to fill those gaps and to validate it ('curation'). We need the ability to manipulate that information, apply it, and turn it into something of value ('creation'). And then we must sell our new creation to our colleagues and customers, wrapping it in a compelling story ('communication').

Leaders augmented with these tools and skills will be well placed to drive decision-making from an informed position. Those who still rely on armies of analysts to wrangle answers from awkward data sets will be at a distinct disadvantage. Follow these steps to ensure you are in the former category:

- **Assess:** Check how your reports, budgets and forecasts are produced. Is it with the proper tools or a tangle of spreadsheets? Is the process well documented or stored in the head of a single individual? How much faith do the people producing the reports have in the data sources they are drawing from?
- **Systematize:** Ensure that processes are documented and any spreadsheets and reports are standardized so that anyone with the relevant skills can understand them.
- **Software:** Look at reporting and CPM software that can begin to automate budgeting, forecasting and reporting processes and open up business inquiries to a wider field of people through a more intuitive user interface. This is not an expensive forklift upgrade of existing systems but an overlay of relatively cheap software to tackle these particular issues.
- **Skills:** Open up skills training around core concepts of analysis and presentation, as well as use of the new software, to a wider range of people. Make it a standard part of training for anyone on a leadership track.

3.4 Communicating Change

Human beings are frequently much more compelled by story than by evidence. For all the talk of evidence-driven decision-making, many neuroscientists have argued that there are no truly rational decisions. Instead, we decide based on emotions and heuristics developed over millions of years of evolution. Then we post-rationalize, fitting the evidence to the decisions we have already made.

Personally, I like to believe that, given time to make decisions, we can at least steer our emotional judgement with evidence and reason, so attempts to improve our rational decision-making are not futile. But it would not be rational or smart for us as leaders to ignore the evidence of the power of emotions in decision-making, or the role that stories can play in swaying those emotions. However great the evidence at our disposal, we are unlikely to be able to steer our organizations effectively if we cannot wrap evidence in a narrative that compels action from our people, our customers and our other stakeholders and partners.

This is why storytelling is such an important skill in the future-proof business. The ability of leaders to tell stories to compel change is a critical part of an organization's ability to respond at speed to high-frequency change. To help leaders tell stories I created a simple tool for this narrative planning. I call the tool 'Arcs'.

Stories of tomorrow

Arcs has two purposes: first, to help you to translate the evidence you have seen – either from your foresight process or from the operational information described in section 3.3 – into action; second, to begin to couch that plan in language that engages stakeholders and catalyses change. It is a process to help you structure and tell a story – a story of tomorrow. It will not make you a more compelling speaker or give a rhetorical flourish to your language – I am afraid you will have to look elsewhere for guidance on that front – but I find that getting from challenge to solution, and from idea to story, is a large part of the problem. And this is where Arcs should help.

CASE STUDY

The future of energy

A few years ago I was commissioned to write a report on the future of the energy sector in the UK. This is a complex industry with many stakeholders that is likely to undergo radical change over the next few years. Here, Arcs was enormously useful.

Intersections provided the core material for the report, highlighting the key pressure points and the likely impacts of the incoming macro trends. But it was Arcs that allowed me to write and later present this report in a way that could easily be understood by all the different audiences, from specialist regulatory lawyers to generating companies to industrial consumers of energy.

By telling a story that started at the beginning – showing a clear understanding of where the industry is today – and then taking each audience through its transformation, I was able to create a report that was both credible and compelling. One lawyer in the audience said to me afterwards: 'I have been in this industry for eighteen years and there are still things I don't understand. You seem to have grasped it all in just six weeks.'

My understanding was obviously relatively narrow compared with his. But Intersections and Arcs had enabled me to latch on to the critical points and identify where the industry should be going, quickly.

Like every story, Arcs stories have a beginning, a middle and an end. At each stage you must answer a series of questions, summarized in the table.

Beginning	Middle	End
What change is coming? What is the context in which that change will happen?	What actions are you going to take to respond to the change? Who will be affected by those actions? How will they be affected?	What is your expected outcome from your actions?

The beginning

Your Arcs story, like every story, is about change. And it starts with the impetus for that change.

This impetus might come from the Intersections process from the second part of this book. What future event or trend have you foreseen to which you now need to respond? The source could also be any other business issue or opportunity that requires you to take a strategic decision and make a plan of action.

Either way, start your story with a description of this impetus. The critical thing to capture here is what is changing.

- Is it customer behaviour?
- Is it market competition?
- Is it process or technology?
- Is it regulation?

Your description doesn't need to be more than a sentence or two, or even just a few words. See if you can work out which industries these situations refer to:

- 'New, digital-native competitors are emerging and beating us on customer service.'
- 'The market is demanding daily small deliveries and we are scaled for weekly, large deliveries.'
- 'New technologies are emerging that will automate much of our daily work.'
- 'Our margins are already thin and new regulations are increasing the cost of our product.'[9]

Context

The next thing you must do is describe the environment into which this impetus will arrive. What is the situation today?

The natural answer to this is to give the usual trading summaries: revenues and profits, and the trends in those numbers over time. How is the balance sheet looking? These facts are useful in laying out the general picture, but in this case we need to be more specific. We need to home in on the factors that are particularly relevant to the impetus that has driven you to undertake this storytelling exercise. You need to make a broad assessment of the readiness of your company to respond. If it is an industry-wide issue, then you may also need to consider how well placed the industry might be to respond. This is not about working out a solution, it is simply understanding which aspects of your business may have to change as part of that solution.

Don't think too hard about the solution or the plan at this stage. If you understand the impetus, then you probably already have an idea of what a response might look like. But even if you do not, you can understand what domain the response might exist in.

For example:

- Is it a marketing issue, around brand or pricing?
- Is it an innovation challenge, around developing a new product or service?
- Is it a customer service opportunity?
- Or is it an internal issue, around process, technology or infrastructure?

Once you have a rough idea of the domain – or domains – that might be involved in any response, you can begin to look at your readiness to develop and execute such a response. List all these critical aspects of the business – and any others that are relevant to your challenge. Highlight the ones that might be most critical to realizing any plan. Now give each one a score from 1 to 10 in terms of your rough assessment of its capability to meet the challenge ahead.

Domain	Readiness (1–10)
Skills: Do you have skills relevant to the challenge inside the organization or in existing partners today?	
(Management) Will: Is the management team engaged and motivated in tackling the challenges presented?	
(Market) Readiness: Is the market ready for change in response to the motivations presented?	
Infrastructure: Do you have the right infrastructure, and the right amount of it, for the challenge at hand?	
Capital: Change can be expensive. Can you fund it?	
(Human) Resource: Are there enough people in the relevant tiers of the organization, or perhaps a surfeit in the wrong ones?	

You can revisit these scores once you have a plan. But it is a valuable exercise to see how much confidence you have in each function without further research. Do you know these functions well enough to give an answer? That in itself might be a good spur for some investigation.

Starting the story
What you should now have is the context for your story. You should be able to say where you are today, what is changing

and how ready you are to face that change. Now you have two choices.

If the challenge is clear, and you understand what it must deliver, you can jump to the end of your story. In some ways it is easier to plot the middle of your narrative arc if you understand where it must end. Whether it is the establishment of market dominance or just a return to profit, you may have a clear objective in mind. Jump to the end now and then return to the middle to work out how you might get there.

If there is less clarity about what the destination might look like, then take things one step at a time. Move to the middle and begin to work out a plan. Then from there you can begin to visualize a destination.

The middle: action

How will you get from the beginning of the story to the end? Whether or not you have yet determined your goal, you can now begin to work out a plan of action in response to the impetus facing you.

Determining the right course of action is a huge step and there is a limit to how much a simple toolkit for storytelling can encapsulate all of the various arguments. But it can be valuable to sketch out the story you will tell for each possible course of action as a way of balancing your options. Try working through the template below for each possible strategy and see how it affects the different audiences. Ensure that any actions listed are true actions and not vague statements of intent. You need to be clear about what will be done, even if you can't specify responsibility and deadlines at this stage.

One way to start to list options is to come back to your context and the rough assessments of your company's capabilities. Where are your strengths? What solutions do these strengths suggest in the face of the impetus?

- High market readiness combined with the available skills and capital might suggest that now is the time to bring a new product or service to market.
- Skills or infrastructure holding the company back would suggest investment or the sourcing of new partners to address opportunities or threats.
- Low scores for management will mean there is an internal communications piece to take on.

Audiences

In narrative planning, you must always consider the effect of your actions on each audience. When they hear this story, they need to know what it means for them. Every organization has multiple audiences, each of which is a stakeholder in the organization's performance. Some that you should consider are listed in the table.

Customers	This will be a diverse group. If necessary, subdivide them using personas. Are they big spenders? Frequent or infrequent buyers? What product set do they buy?
Staff	Staff in different lines of business and functions will have different perspectives. Consider breaking them down into subgroups.

Partners/ Suppliers	How will the people on either side of your supply chain be affected? There are likely different effects depending on their scale, products and services, and the nature of their interactions with you.
Owners/ Investors	This might include shareholders, parent companies and board members, each with their own perspective and objectives.
Regulators	You are probably overseen by at least two or three different government bodies or independent regulators. What will their perspective be on the change?

When you are determining which possible courses of action to take, consider the most important audiences. Who is likely to be most affected, given the motivation and the strengths and weaknesses that are to be addressed?

Impact

The next stage of this process requires you to understand the impact that each action or intervention might have. This impact is rarely felt in just one place. There is the intended impact on the organization, usually an adjustment designed to make the operation fitter for the future: reducing costs, creating new products, etc. But there are additional impacts on specific audiences.

Think about all the stakeholders in your client's organization identified in the last section. Shareholders or citizens, staff and partners, suppliers and resellers. Each intervention may have an impact in any or every one of these groups.

It is rare that interventions have uniquely positive or negative effects on these audiences. In many cases they have both. For example, a new share issue to raise capital in support of planned changes may dilute the holdings of existing investors (negative), but it may also give them the chance to increase their investment at a preferred rate (positive) and bring in new shareholders (positive).

The end: objectives

The end of the story is your destination. Where is this journey that started with the impetus going to lead you? What does the new land of milk and honey, or maybe just survival, look like? Try to describe the world after your intervention. What does sustainable success look like? This is the place for the broad brushstrokes: financial security, growth, improved customer satisfaction, better environmental performance. Down the line you can flesh this out with targets and metrics. But at this stage you are simply setting out your ambition.

Your story template

What should be becoming clear is that there are many versions of your future story. Each stakeholder will have a different perspective based on the impact of your likely interventions. The next stage of the process is to synthesize a series of statements based on the content gathered so far that, together, form the basis of the story. It's impossible to craft a truly poetic narrative in such a systematic way, but these statements should form a strong foundation onto which you can build.

It starts with the beginning:

- Change is coming to our [COMPANY/INDUSTRY] driven by [IMPETUS].
- This change comes in a context of [COMPANY/INDUSTRY STRENGTHS/WEAKNESSES].

This is followed by your action and the intended objective:

- In response to this change we plan to [ACTION] in order to secure [OBJECTIVE].

It ends with a description of the impact for each audience:

- For [AUDIENCE] this will mean [POSITIVE IMPACT] and/or [NEGATIVE IMPACT].

Clearly, there won't always be a positive and a negative impact so one of these can often be removed. The positions may also be reversed, depending on what is the most appropriate emphasis. You will likely end up with multiple audience statements.

Qualify and polish

As your narrative starts to take shape you can begin to do two things.

The first is to add qualification. Add richness, depth and justification, perhaps using the evidence discovered about current issues or the impetus in the Intersections process. The second is to polish the rather robotic statements into something a little more poetic. These stories are only valuable in helping the company to make change if they can compel people into action. You may be equipped to add the necessary rhetorical flair for this, but it may be the job of an experienced communicator and copywriter to take the statements you have crafted and produce something that reads as a coherent, convincing story that people can buy into. The key tip here is to ensure that whatever you produce sounds like you or, even better, sounds like your audience.

Once you have produced your narrative for each of the audiences that matter, the next step is to take it to them and make the case for change. Few organizations change easily. In fact, the ability to change has been engineered out of many organizations by years of focused optimization on single markets, products or tasks.

3.5 Next Steps

Future-proof businesses are athletic businesses. Like great athletes they:

- sense the world acutely,
- take decisions quickly,
- train for agility.

How do you make your business into one with these characteristics? Here are some good first steps.

Step 1: Make time

You do not spend time looking to the future today because you probably do not have the time to spend. So, the first thing you need to do is to make time for you and for the people who support you. That means creating a culture of devolved power. Release some responsibility. If you have put good people around you, they can take it. But only if they too release some responsibility. And so on, down the hierarchy.

Some people will come to you saying that they need to invest to release time. These investments will be in areas that have been unfashionable in recent years because they are not directly customer-facing. They might be investments in skills training, coaching or development. They might be in human resource to create time to build rules and processes. Perhaps they will be in systems to automate some of the current workload. These are usually good investments and they are often critical to building sustainable success. They can also often be relatively small investments. Create a pot for investment in this type of ongoing development that people can bid to access.

Step 2: Start to scan the horizon

Now that you have created some time, you need to devote at least 1 per cent of your total hours to scanning the horizon. That is roughly one day every six months spent examining the pressures you currently face and the trends coming your way. Use the Intersections process as laid out in part 2. Make sure you engage with lots of other opinions and perspectives in this process from both inside and outside the company. Seek out peers and partners as well as people at every level in the organization.

Every couple of years, make time to look a bit further out and use the scenario-planning tool to imagine the world we are entering. Reset your goals and objectives against this new world and look for any preventative steps you can take for whatever might be coming.

Step 3: Accelerate delegation

Continue the process started in Step 1 of pushing power out to the edges of the organization. Establish this as a core element of company culture from the top down and empower people across the business to give and to take power where they can add value by doing so. Support initiatives with training and coaching, and ensure that there is clarity around the rules and boundaries within which people operate. Adopt as a principle that power should be devolved unless there is a good reason not to.

Step 4: Improve information flow

Look at the accessibility of good information used to drive decisions. Everyone in your organization who needs data to make decisions should have access both to those data and to the skills and tools necessary to manipulate and analyse it. Look at systems, policies and training to address these issues while being mindful of any restrictions around privacy and regulation.

Step 5: Structure for agility

Function by function, begin to break your business down into units, or building blocks, as in section 1.3. You can work layer by layer, based on the model in section 1.4. Or you can start with any functions that raised issues in the pressure points section of Intersections in section 2.4. Engage the team in the process – indeed, it should be led by the function leader. Look for gaps and inefficiencies. Encourage each function to begin to think and operate entrepreneurially. And if that opportunity doesn't exist, consider if that unit fits under your corporate umbrella. Most of all, look at the interfaces between functions, and between you and your partners, and you and your customers. Eliminate bad friction, increase good friction.

It's all about change

Being future-proof means not standing still. Not assuming that what makes for a successful business today will continue to ensure a successful business tomorrow. So, every process in this book is iterative. It never stops. This is why there is so much focus on delegation and creating the time for strategic thought and action. Because agility and change *is* the business of management now. Optimization is the role of people close to the action. Leaders must lead change. It comes back to the analogy of the athlete. The greatest sportspeople are not necessarily the ones with the most technical skill or talent. They are the ones with the vision. The footballer who always looks up to spot that critical pass. The runner who knows their opponent and times their break perfectly. In an age of high-frequency change, the leaders who build future-proof businesses will be the ones who keep their heads up and focused on tomorrow.

Acknowledgements

This book wouldn't exist without the feedback from and interactions with my clients over the last few years. You have helped to shape my thinking and progressively simplify and tighten up these processes to get them into the shape in which they appear in this book. Too many have contributed to this project in different ways for me to name everyone, but I am particularly grateful to Simon King for being an early believer in the value I could bring. To Ben Rachel for his frank feedback and his willingness always to bat ideas about over a few beers. And to James Hanson, my former colleague, client and friend, who has been a supporter of this project from the beginning.

Notes

Part 1: How to Structure a Future-proof Business

1 https://corpgov.law.harvard.edu/2018/02/12/ceo-tenure-rates/

2 https://www2.staffingindustry.com/eng/Editorial/Daily-News/UK-CEO-turnover-falls-to-10-as-internal-candidates-are-promoted-Robert-Half-50249

3 If you are in a leadership position today and have not overworked yourself at some point, then you either work in a truly progressive organization, or you are much smarter than me. One might even say, devious.

4 https://scm.ncsu.edu/scm-articles/article/a-brief-history-of-outsourcing

5 Alexander Osterwalder, *Business Model Generation: A Handbook for Visionaries, Game Changers and Challengers.* John Wiley & Sons, 2010.

6 In Greek myth, Sisyphus was condemned by Zeus to endlessly roll a rock up a hill as a punishment for tricking the gods.

7 https://www.mckinsey.com/industries/retail/our-insights/the-three-cs-of-customer-satisfaction-consistency-consistency-consistency

8 https://blogs.gartner.com/jake-sorofman/in-customer-experience-consistency-is-the-new-delight/

Part 2: How to See the Future

1 McKinsey & Company, 'Pulp, paper, and packaging in the next decade: Transformational change'. https://www.mckinsey.com/~/media/McKinsey/Industries/Paper%20and%20Forest%20Products/Our%20Insights/Pulp%20paper%20and%20packaging%20in%20the%20next%20decade%20Transformational%20change/Pulp-paper-and-packaging-in-the-next-decade-Transformational-change-2019-vF.ashx

2 https://www.h3uni.org/practices/foresight-three-horizons/. See also Bill Sharpe, *Three Horizons: The Patterning of Hope*, Triarchy Press, 2013.

3 Deloitte, Ernst & Young, KPMG and PricewaterhouseCoopers.

4 John P. Kotter, *Leading Change* (new edn), Harvard Business Review Press, 2012.

5 https://www.mckinsey.com/business-functions/organization/our-insights/how-to-beat-the-transformation-odds

6 https://www.forbes.com/sites/blakemorgan/2019/09/30/companies-that-failed-at-digital-transformation-and-what-we-can-learn-from-them/#76cc00ed603c

7 Economist Joseph Schumpeter coined this term to describe the way free-market competition creates an endless cycle of building up and knocking down of companies, which ultimately – at least in theory – leads to progress: https://www.econlib.org/library/Enc/CreativeDestruction.html

8 Organisation for Economic Co-operation and Development https://commonslibrary.parliament.uk/economy-business/economy-economy/recession-and-recovery-the-german-experience/

Part 3: Rapid Response

1   Captured in Kahneman's award-winning book *Thinking, Fast and Slow*, Penguin, 2012, published after Tversky's death.

2   https://audit.future-of-finance.com/

3   https://www.statista.com/statistics/386763/aldi-sales-percentage-change-great-britain-uk/

4   https://targetjobs.co.uk/career-sectors/retail-buying-and-merchandising/320929-application-and-interview-advice-for-aldi-s-area-management-graduate

5   https://journals.sagepub.com/doi/pdf/10.1177/0730888417697232

6   Ann Francke, *Create a Gender-balanced Workplace*, Penguin, 2019.

7   https://www.pwc.com/mu/pwc-22nd-annual-global-ceo-survey-mu.pdf

8   http://dresneradvisory.com/blog/a-new-maturity-model-for-the-digital-enterprise-10928

9   Respectively, banking, retail logistics, professional services including law and accounting, and residential construction.

Index

PENGUIN PARTNERSHIPS

Penguin Partnerships is the Creative Sales and Promotions team at Penguin Random House. We have a long history of working with clients on a wide variety of briefs, specializing in brand promotions, bespoke publishing and retail exclusives, plus corporate, entertainment and media partnerships.

We can respond quickly to briefs and specialize in repurposing books and content for sales promotions, for use as incentives and retail exclusives as well as creating content for new books in collaboration with our partners as part of branded book relationships.

Equally if you'd simply like to buy a bulk quantity of one of our existing books at a special discount, we can help with that too. Our books can make excellent corporate or employee gifts.

Special editions, including personalized covers, excerpts of existing books or books with corporate logos can be created in large quantities for special needs.

We can work within your budget to deliver whatever you want, however you want it.

For more information, please contact
salesenquiries@penguinrandomhouse.co.uk